Alun Lewis

COLLECTED POEMS

The Uniform Edition of
Alun Lewis's Writings

Letters to My Wife
Collected Stories

Alun Lewis

COLLECTED POEMS

Edited by Cary Archard

seren

Seren is the book imprint of
Poetry Wales Press Ltd
Nolton Street, Bridgend
CF31 3AE
Wales
www.seren-books.com

First published in 1994
First paperback edition: 2007

A CIP record for this title is available at the
British Library CIP Office

ISBN 1-85411-316-X
ISBN 978-1-85411-316-0

The publisher works with the financial support of the Welsh Books Council

Printed in Palatino by Bell & Bain Ltd, Glasgow

Contents

UNCOLLECTED POEMS

Biographical Table: Alun Lewis 1915-1944

1915   *1 July*. Alun Lewis born at 16 Llanwynno Road, Cwmaman, near Aberdare, south Wales, son of Tom and Gwladys Lewis, both teachers.

1917   Glyn Lewis, second son, born. (Huw born in 1919, Mair in 1921.)

1918   Tom Lewis wounded in the leg and discharged from the army.

1920   Alun starts school at Glynhafod Infants.

1925   Summer holiday at Penbryn on the Cardiganshire coast; subsequently the family holiday there regularly in August. Becomes one of Alun's favourite places.

1926   Alun wins scholarship to the Grammar School at Cowbridge, a boarding school twenty miles away in the Vale of Glamorgan. Often homesick, isolated and unhappy. But encouraged by Eric Reid, his English teacher, Alun becomes an enthusiastic sportsman and debater, and contributes six remarkable short stories to the school magazine, *The Bovian*. Influenced by Reid's liberal ideas, and by his pacifist and anti-imperialist attitudes.

1932-35   Alun attends University College of Wales, Aberystwyth. He boxes, plays hockey for the First XI and writes for college revues. Fully involved in student life. His writing develops through short stories for *The Dragon*, the college magazine, which also publishes a sonnet, 'The Ladybird Wakes'. Awarded First Class Honours in History.
31 August 1935. Another sonnet, 'On the Death of Queen Astrid' appears in the *Western Mail*.

1935   *September*. Awarded Postgraduate Studentship at University of Manchester. Thesis on the work of thirteenth century Papal Legate, Ottobono. Lives in Chorlton, a gloomy part of what he sees as a gloomy city. An introspective period, the first of a number, in which Alun becomes depressed and isolated. Stories and poems in the university magazine, *The Serpent*, one of which, 'The Pattern', includes 'O have you seen the thorn that grows'.

1937   *May*. Visits Pontigny in northern France for nine weeks, at a student conference on European politics run by Catholic philosopher Paul Desjardines. At talks and discussions considers his own positions on politics and culture.
September. Returns to Aberystwyth for teacher training course, having considered the civil service and librarianship.

1938   More stories and poems in *The Dragon*. Poems also appear in *The Observer* and *Time and Tide* which publishes 'Poems from the Chinese'.
Alun applies unsuccessfully for teaching and journalism posts.
August. Tours Normandy for two weeks with college friend Richard Mills.
September. Works unofficially at *The Aberdare Leader* to which he contributes a number of articles about the political situation in Europe, including 'If War Comes – Will I Fight?'.
Reads some of his poems from the BBC studio in Cardiff.
November. Takes a temporary teaching post at Lewis Boys' School, Pengam.

1939   *May*. Meets Gweno Ellis, a teacher at Mountain Ash Grammar School, just south of Aberdare. Makes unsuccessful attempt to have collection of short stories published.
Summer. Works on unpublished novel, *Morlais*, about a miner's son growing up in Cwmaman.
November. Appointed permanent member of staff at Pengam, where he is highly popular with the boys. Sees more and more of Gweno as year progresses.

1940   Works on unpublished novel, *Adam*, about student life in Aberystwyth.
March. Hurts hand quite badly in classroom accident. Spends time with Gweno at her parents' home in Aberystwyth and on holidays in north Wales and the Gower.
15 May. After much self-questioning, impulsively decides to

enlist and joins the Royal Engineers in London, anxious to avoid killing a man. Sent to No. 1 Railway Training Centre at Longmoor, Hants. Army life (fatigues and boredom of repetitive training) shocks him. Writing flows, especially poetry; writes 'The Soldier', 'The Public Gardens', 'Raider's Dawn'. The short story, 'Lance Jack', appears in *Life and Letters*.

October. Visits Edward Thomas's house at Steep. Thomas's poetry and personality deeply affect him and he writes 'All day it has rained' and 'To Edward Thomas'. Finds educational role and organizes lectures, debates and a reading room.

1941   *Spring.* Meets the artist John Petts, whose engraving of Alun later appears on the cover of *Raiders' Dawn*. Alun, Petts and his wife Brenda Chamberlain produce a series of broadsheets, each containing poems and illustrations. He writes about "Two urgent needs for me: one to write for: the other, to educate *The People*". Six Caseg Broadsheets appear between November 1941 and June 1942. Alun's story 'They Came' wins the Edward J. O'Brien Short Story Award.

5 July. Alun marries Gweno Ellis in Gloucester while attending an officer training course.

11 July. Posted to the Officer Cadet Training Unit at Heysham Towers, near Morecambe, Lancashire. Writes the long poem, 'War Wedding'. Allen & Unwin accept his poems for publication.

31 October. Leaves Heysham a promising Second Lieutenant.

4 November. Begins correspondence with Robert Graves.

29 November. Alun joins Sixth Battalion of the South Wales Borderers at Woodbridge, Suffolk, after a long leave. Finds company of senior officers uncongenial but is happier with men of his platoon, most of whom come from south Wales.

December. Alun's work discussed in article on English poets in *Lilliput*.

1942   *March. Raiders' Dawn*, his first book of poems, is published to general acclaim and is reprinted three times that year.

Borderers move to Orwell Park. Alun sent to the battle school at Aldeburgh: the stories, 'Acting Captain' and 'Cold Spell' written at this time. Allen & Unwin agree to publish a collection of his stories.

May. Borderers sent for tank training at Bovington, Dorset. Alun learns engine mechanics and radio telegraphy. After a visit to Cloud Hills, where T.E. Lawrence had lived, he writes 'Dusty Hermitage', one of the best stories in *The Last Inspection*.

August. The Borderers move to Southend.

October, month end, Borderers posted to India. Sail on *Athlone Castle* from Liverpool, where Alun and Gweno spend their last night together. As Entertainments Officer, Alun is kept busy organizing concerts, games, debates, etc.

15 November. Reaches Bahia, Brazil.

4 December. Athlone Castle puts into Durban.

17 December. The Battalion arrives at Bombay and travels on to Nira, southeast of Poona. Alun is struck by the pitiless heat, dryness and poverty of India.

1943   *January*. Alun fractures his jaw playing in a regimental football match and spends six weeks in Poona hospital. Undergoes two operations and suffers much pain and intro-spection. Another burst of writing produces poems such as 'In Hospital: Poona (1)', 'In Hospital: Poona (2)', 'Burma Casualty' and the story, 'Ward "O" 3(b)'.

February. *The Last Inspection*, a collection of nineteen stories, mostly written since his enlistment, is published to consider-able critical acclaim.

March. Alun returns to Nira as Intelligence Officer and makes many reconnaissance trips to the Mahratta Hills.

20 March. The battalion joins the 36th Indian Infantry Division at Lake Kharakvasla for training in preparation for offensive against the Japanese in Burma. Creative period continues with the poems 'Village Funeral', 'Home Thoughts from Abroad', 'Bequest', 'Shadows' and 'Water Music', and the short story about the capture of of an Indian nationalist, 'The Raid'.

June. Broadcasts his poems on All-India Radio.

July. Writes 'The Orange Grove', his most ambitious short story, based on reconnaissance journeys north of Bombay.

24 July. On leave at Coonoor in the Nilgiri Hills, visits and falls in love with Freda Aykroyd. Writes 'Ways', 'Wood Song' and 'Beloved Beware'.

4 August. Alun returns to Poona ('The Way Back') en route to the Military Intelligence School in Karachi. Turns down promotion to staff officer. He wishes to remain close to his men and share their dangers.

September. Freda and Alun spend five days together in Bombay before he rejoins his battalion. Writes 'Pastorals', 'Renewal', 'Lady in Black' and 'A Fragment'.

November. Alun suffers an attack of malaria: Poona hospital again for a week.

December. Meets his brother Glyn in Poona on leave. Results in the short story, 'The Reunion'.

1944   *January*. 'The Jungle', his last poem.

After taking Robert Graves's advice, Alun revises his poems for his second collection which he decides to title ironically, *Ha! Ha! Among the Trumpets*, (a quote from Job 39).

13 February. The Borderers leave Poona by rail for Calcutta, then proceed by boat via Chittagong to Cox's Bazar in north Burma. By the month end Alun writes his last letter to Gweno as the battalion moves to Bawli, behind the front line.

4 March. Alun requests to join B Company at Goppe Pass at the front.

5 March. Early morning, after shaving and washing, Alun is found shot in the head near the officers' latrines. His revolver found in his hand. He dies of the wound six hours later, and is buried the same day at Bawli military cemetery.

31 March. An army court of enquiry concludes the shooting was an accident.

1945   *August. Ha! Ha! Among the Trumpets* published.

1946   *Letters from India*, edited by Gweno Lewis and Gwyn Jones.

1948   *In the Green Tree*, short stories and letters from India, illustrated by John Petts.

Introduction

Alun Lewis and Keith Douglas are generally recognized to be the two outstanding poets of the Second World War. However, whereas Douglas's collected poems have been readily available, Lewis's remarkable body of work has been strangely neglected.

Most of Alun Lewis's poems, and nearly all those he wanted to see published in book form, appeared in his two collections. An editor, I feel, ought to respect the poet's own judgement as far as possible, and this is especially important in the case of Lewis who took such pains over the organisation of his collections. Accordingly this *Collected Poems* includes the complete texts of his two published books, *Raiders' Dawn* (1942) and *Ha! Ha! Among the Trumpets* (1945), reprinted in chronological order and retaining the important original section headings under which Lewis chose to arrange and group his poetry.

Lewis's two collections are a remarkably detailed and full account of the experience of becoming a soldier and going to war. Nearly all of the poems were written between September 1939 and January 1944 and practically all of them were written on active service. Not simply a record of his war, Lewis's poems are also, as the organisation of his books underlines, a young man's earnest struggle to make sense of all that was happening to him, to begin with in his soldier training in England and then in his journey closer to the theatre of war in India. He was especially preoccupied with the conflict between the creative act of writing poetry and what he saw as the brutalising and destructive nature of soldiering. For Lewis the gift of poetry was a heavy responsibility. He wanted to get things right – in the sense of being true to that gift. No-one can read this collection of poems, together in one volume for the first time, without being struck by how the singularity of his voice permeates a surprising diversity of forms. Most readers of his work have commented on the essential honesty and integrity of his writing. When it came to completing *Ha! Ha! Among the Trumpets*, to get that right, Lewis consulted Robert Graves, the contemporary poet he most admired: "I was a bit bothered lest the poems and your notes arrived too late for me to do the necessary revising, but I've manged it in the nick. For both your purgative criticism and your general fiat I am more grateful than I can say". In these last poems, Lewis was still experimenting, trying to find the right register for his intense lyrical voice. As he wrote with typically percep- tive self-criticism to his sister Mair about the poems: "I think they are less rhetorical and more straight spoken and less influenced by schools or by poets, but more guarded and objective, less ambitious".

Besides presenting for the general reader Lewis's two books in their entirety, this *Collected* includes twenty-seven more poems, fifteen of which have been published before in books which are now unavailable. When Ian Hamilton produced his pioneering *Alun Lewis: Selected Poetry and Prose* (1966), he included eight fine poems which had never been published: 'Southend at Dusk', 'Bequest', 'The River Temple: Wai', 'The Run-In', 'The Patrol', 'Lady in Black', 'Indolence' and 'Sonnet for Gweno'. Fifteen years later, the unpublished poems, 'Renewal' and 'Pastorals' were included by Jeremy Hooker and Gweno Lewis in their *Selected Poems of Alun Lewis*. And in 1982 among much uncollected writing (prose and poetry), John Pikoulis, Alun Lewis's biographer, included the unpublished poems, 'On Leave: Marriage' and 'The Soubrettes', and three previously unpublished poems 'On the Welsh Mountains' (*Poems from the Forces*), 'Prelude and Fugue' and 'The Suicide' (both from *Tribune*), in his *Alun Lewis: A Miscellany of his Writings*.

The remaining twelve poems (most of which are included here to give the reader an idea of Lewis's earliest work) have two main sources. Two, 'Song, Oh have you seen the thorn' and 'The Quest' appeared in *The Observer* (1937 and 1938), a newspaper which generously encouraged the twenty-two years old student poet by taking no fewer than seven of his early poems, most of which were published in student magazines by the two universities Lewis attended. Nine poems are taken from a manuscript collection of around sixty unpublished poems, most of which were written before the poems in *Raiders' Dawn*, kept among the Alun Lewis Papers in the National Library of Wales in Aberystwyth. Of these the earliest is 'The Slug' (1935-36) and one of the most remarkable is 'The Tiger of Camden Town'

(1938). Poems such as these seem very modern now (post-war rather than pre-war) and suggest very different directions Lewis's poetry might have taken had the war not intervened. 'The Swimmer' (1939) and 'Greetings' (1940) are poems that Lewis might have felt were too personal for his first collection. Only two of the twelve poems were written after *Raiders' Dawn*. 'Beloved Beware' was written in August 1943 in India. 'Letter From the Cape' is one of the two poems (the other, 'Letter From a Long Way', is not included here) Lewis agonised over when he was putting the finishing touches to *Ha! Ha! Among the Trumpets*. He wrote to Robert Graves: "I couldn't decide myself – they are too much flesh of my flesh for me to pretend to assess them: and I've left it to Gweno to exclude them if she chooses. I feel myself that they are necessary to the book: they establish certain things about myself which belong organically to the poems as a whole". In the event, Gweno respected her husband's uncertainty and the poems did not appear in the book.

The editor is grateful to Gweno Lewis for allowing him to publish 'Letter From The Cape' for the first time. He is also grateful to Gweno and her late brother Hywel for their support, encouragement and help in the preparation of this volume.

Acknowledgements

Acknowledgements are due to Gweno Lewis for permission to reprint the poems of Alun Lewis. For poems from The Alun Lewis Papers the editor acknowledges the permission of The National Library of Wales, Aberystwyth.

Raiders' Dawn
and other poems

Prologue: The Grinder

Nothing to grind? Then answer, and I'll go.
Who carved the round red sun?
Who purified the snow?
Who is that hidden one? You do not know.

Then, as you cannot answer, I will take
Such odds and ends as likely you possess,
And grind them fine and patch them for their sake
And other reasons which you may not guess.

I grind my words like knives on such events
As I encounter in my peddling round.
But the worn whetstone's whirling face prevents
The perfect statement of the truths I found.

I've used my strength in striving for the vision,
And *with* the vision – like old Jacob's stress;
And I have worked to outline with precision
Existence in its native nakedness.

But why should a grinder of words be counted much?
His patched umbrellas and his notched old knives,
His makeshift stone and lathe – who values such
A stroller through ten thousand petty lives?

Who carved the round red sun? The sun has set.
Who purified the snow? The hills are white.
Keep grinding then, though nothing's left to whet –
Bad luck unless your sparks can warm the night.

Poems in Khaki

Raiders' Dawn

Softly the civilized
Centuries fall,
Paper on paper,
Peter on Paul.

And lovers waking
From the night –
Eternity's masters,
Slaves of Time –
Recognize only
The drifting white
Fall of small faces
In pits of lime.

Blue necklace left
On a charred chair
Tells that Beauty
Was startled there.

All Day It Has Rained...

All day it has rained, and we on the edge of the moors
Have sprawled in our bell-tents, moody and dull as boors,
Groundsheets and blankets spread on the muddy ground
And from the first grey wakening we have found
No refuge from the skirmishing fine rain
And the wind that made the canvas heave and flap
And the taut wet guy-ropes ravel out and snap.
All day the rain has glided, wave and mist and dream,
Drenching the gorse and heather, a gossamer stream
Too light to stir the acorns that suddenly
Snatched from their cups by the wild south-westerly
Pattered against the tent and our upturned dreaming faces.
And we stretched out, unbuttoning our braces,
Smoking a Woodbine, darning dirty socks,
Reading the Sunday papers – I saw a fox
And mentioned it in the note I scribbled home; –
And we talked of girls, and dropping bombs on Rome,
And thought of the quiet dead and the loud celebrities
Exhorting us to slaughter, and the herded refugees;
– Yet thought softly, morosely of them, and as indifferently
As of ourselves or those whom we
For years have loved, and will again
To-morrow maybe love; but now it is the rain
Possesses us entirely, the twilight and the rain.

And I can remember nothing dearer or more to my heart
Than the children I watched in the woods on Saturday
Shaking down burning chestnuts for the schoolyard's merry play,
Or the shaggy patient dog who followed me
By Sheet and Steep and up the wooded scree
To the Shoulder o' Mutton where Edward Thomas brooded long
On death and beauty – till a bullet stopped his song.

The Soldier

I

I within me holding
Turbulence and Time
– Volcanic fires deep beneath the glacier –
Feel the dark cancer in my vitals
Of impotent impatience grope its way
Through daze and dream to throat and fingers
To find its climax of disaster.

The sunlight breaks its flashing wings
Imprisoned in the Hall of Mirrors;
Nightmare rides upon the headlines:
And summer leaves her green reflective woods
To glitter momently on peaks of madness.

But leisurely my fellow soldiers stroll among the trees.
The cheapest dance-song utters all they feel.

II

Now as a lover would
Kiss while walking
In the beech copse
By the chalk-pit
I stand and marvel
At the finches'
Identical beauty
Heraldic markings
Power of wings
To flicker and blossom
On branches of song.

Say that they lust
And squabble and die;
Say their glancing copulation,

Poised flutter on a twig,
Ignores the holy mystery
Of boy and girl together
Timelessly.
                    Yet still
I who am agonized by thought
And war and love
Grow calm again
With watching
The flash and play of finches
Who are as beautiful
And as indifferent to me
As England is, this Spring morning.

The Public Gardens

Only a few top-heavy holly-hocks, wilting in arid beds,
Frayed lawns,
Twin sycamores storing the darkness massively under
        balconies of leaf,
And an empty rococo bandstand – strangely unpopular
Saturday evening in the public gardens.

But wait: These take their places:–

A thin little woman in black stockings and a straw hat with
        wax flowers,
Holding a varnished cane with both hands against her
        spent knees
As she sits alone on the bench, yes oddly
Alone and at rest:

An older wealthier lady, gesticulating and over-dressed,
Puffily reciting the liturgy of vexations
To her beautiful companion,
The remote and attractive demi-Parnassian
Whose dark hair catches the sunlight as she listens
With averted face and apparent understanding:

A boy with his crutches laid against the wall
Pale in the shadow where the hops hang over
In light green bundles; – is he, too, waiting
For one who perhaps
Prefers another?
And I, forgetting my khaki, my crude trade,
And the longing that has vexed and silenced me all the day,
Now simply consider the quiet people,
How their pattern emerges as the evening kindles
Till the park is a maze of diagonal lines, ah far
Too fine to catch the sun like the glittering webs
The spiders have folded and flung from the fading privet.

Only the children, passionately,
Snap my drifting lines with laughter
As they chase each other among the benches
In and out of the dreaming gardens.

The Sentry

I have begun to die.
For now at last I know
That there is no escape
From Night. Not any dream
Nor breathless images of sleep
Touch my bat's-eyes. I hang
Leathery-arid from the hidden roof
Of Night, and sleeplessly
I watch within Sleep's province.
I have left
The lovely bodies of the boy and girl
Deep in each other's placid arms;
And I have left
The beautiful lanes of sleep
That barefoot lovers follow to this last
Cold shore of thought I guard.
I have begun to die
And the guns' implacable silence
Is my black interim, my youth and age,
In the flower of fury, the folded poppy,
Night.

To Edward Thomas

(On visiting the memorial stone above Steep in Hampshire)

I

On the way up from Sheet I met some children
Filling a pram with brushwood; higher still
Beside Steep church an old man pointed out
A rough white stone upon a flinty spur
Projecting from the high autumnal woods....
I doubt if much has changed since you came here
On your last leave; except the stone; it bears
Your name and trade: 'To Edward Thomas, Poet.'

II

Climbing the steep path through the copse I knew
My cares weighed heavily as yours, my gift
Much less, my hope
No more than yours.
And like you I felt sensitive and somehow apart,
Lonely and exalted by the friendship of the wind
And the placid afternoon enfolding
The dangerous future and the smile.

III

I sat and watched the dusky berried ridge
Of yew-trees, deepened by oblique dark shafts,
Throw back the flame of red and gold and russet
That leapt from beech and ash to birch and chestnut
Along the downward arc of the hill's shoulder,
And sunlight with discerning fingers
Softly explore the distant wooded acres,
Touching the farmsteads one by one with lightness
Until it reached the Downs, whose soft green pastures

Went slanting sea- and skywards to the limits
Where sight surrenders and the mind alone
Can find the sheeps' tracks and the grazing.

And for that moment Life appeared
As gentle as the view I gazed upon.

IV

Later, a whole day later, I remembered
This war and yours and your weary
Circle of failure and your striving
To make articulate the groping voices
Of snow and rain and dripping branches
And love that ailing in itself cried out
About the straggling eaves and ringed the candle
With shadows slouching round your buried head;
And in the lonely house there was no ease
For you, or Helen, or those small perplexed
Children of yours who only wished to please.

Divining this, I knew the voice that called you
Was soft and neutral as the sky
Breathing on the grey horizon, stronger
Than night's immediate grasp, the limbs of mercy
Oblivious as the blood; and growing clearer,
More urgent as all else dissolved away,
– Projected books, half-thoughts, the children's birthdays,
And wedding anniversaries as cold
As dates in history – the dream
Emerging from the fact that folds a dream,
The endless rides of stormy-branched dark
Whose fibres are a thread within the hand –

Till suddenly, at Arras, you possessed that hinted land.

'Odi et Amo'

I

Did the fingers of the hand
Touch the sweetest music on
The limbs and lineaments of love
Whose chords resolved in stillness, in the
Stillness of the heart in the white breast?

Did the anxious eyes of pain
Bravely bear the stigmata
Of the christ in us, the livid
Weal of history bleeding in us again?

Did the loins in passion find
Divinity in substance, and in heat
A flame that gathered all eternity
Into the milky ways of night?

And did not hands and eyes and loins
Vow when this cruel deed began
Fiercely blindly to endure
With all the stubborn faith of man

The terrible anguish of the birth
That could not be prevented and the death
That must die, and the peace
That was dreamed of in the beginning?

II

My body does not seem my own
Now. These hands are not my own
That touch the hair-spring trigger, nor my eyes
Fixed on a human target, nor my cheek
Stroking the rifle butt; my loins
Are flat and closed like a child's.

III

Yet in this blood-soaked forest of disease
Where wolfish men lie scorched and black
And corpses sag against the trees
And love's dark roots writhe back

Like snakes into the scorching earth;
In this corrupted wood where none can hear
The love songs of Ophelia
And the laughter of Lear,

My soul cries out with love
Of all that walk and swim and fly.
From the mountains, from the sky,
Out of the depths of the sea
Love cries and cries in me.

And summer blossoms break above my head
With all the unbearable beauty of the dead.

Lines on a Tudor Mansion

Slim sunburnt girls adorn
Lawns browsed by fawn and doe
Through three long centuries this house
Has mellowed in and known
Only the seasonal fulfilment
And the commemorated generations.

But *we* know
Samson dead
And Delilah dirtying her hair
In the dust of the fallen
Faiths.

We know
Violence terrible and degrading,
Beauty disfigured,
And the coward cruel brute
Shaping us in his image.

So, grey assured house, surviving change,
For all your cypresses and waving white
Potato rows and clustered irises, no more
Than woodpecker or mouse do we desire
Your burnished peace and all your storied past.

We are of Life,
Teeming and musical
Perfect and instant
As the soft silk flash of the swifts
Which do not care for the houses of the wealthy,
But have instead their own instinctive life,
The flight and rhythm of the blood.

Wherefore we leave no monumental homes,
No marble cenotaphs inscribed with names.

Only the fleeting sunlight in the forest,
And dragonflies' blue flicker on quiet pools
Will perpetuate our vision

Who die young.

To a Comrade in Arms

Red fool, my laughing comrade,
Hiding your woman's love
And your man's madness,
Patrolling farther than nowhere
To gain what is nearer than here,
Your face will grow grey as Christ's garments
With the dust of ditches and trenches.
So endlessly faring.

Red fool, my laughing comrade,
Hiding your mystic symbols
Of bread broken for eating
And palm-leaves strewn for welcome,
 What foe will you make your peace with
This summer that is more cruel
Than the ancient God of the Hebrews?

When bees swarm in your nostrils
And honey drips from the sockets
Of eyes that to-day are frantic
With love that is frustrate,

What vow shall we vow who love you
For the self you did not value?

Finale

He who continually struck poses
By the palm-tree in the foyer,
At the saloon bar and the banker's counter,
Crossing the dance floor after the rumba;
Who saw himself glorified in the minds of others,
Was fascinating to the young ladies,
Male, seductive, sardonic for the occasion;
Whose sloping shoulders were blazoned for duration
With the flashy epaulettes of tradition,
And yet was ever restless in ambition,
Locked in uneasy conflict with the unwinking
Inscrutable demon of self-knowledge;

Today he struck a final gesture,
Arms akimbo against the sky,
Crucified on a cross of fire
With all the heroic age magnificent in him.

And now he lies in a pose more rigid
Than any that Life with its gambler's chance
Flung on him at a venture.

He had no choice in this, yet seems content
That Life's confused dishonesty
Should find this last simplicity.

The Defeated: for Wales

'Sooner will his blood be spent than he go to the wedding feast.
No hatred shall there be between thee and me; better will I do to thee,
        to praise thee in song.'
                    (A Welsh Poem – 7th-9th century.)

Our courage is an old legend.
We left the fields of our fathers.
Fate was our foeman.

We held the world in our fingers
And threw it like a farthing
That needed no keeping.

More love was there never
By Euphrates and Tigris
Than in our proud country.

Love was our talisman.
We were blinded in battle
By the weeping of women.

Bled white are our wounds,
Wounds writhing with worms;
All spilt the quick seed....

Oh! dark are we whose greed for life
Was a green slash in our eyes
And in our darkness we are wise,

Forgetting honour, valour, fame,
In this darkness whence we came.

Parable

The soul within his pastoral
Grew ripe as barley in the sun,
Ran with the clear green swiftness of a brook,
Blossomed across the wide and branching sky
And mated simply in the ferns –
Until an inner anguish woke
The horror of his century.
And then he sought within the glades of Love
The bleating wounded beast that was his voice.

His pastoral country was much coveted.
The sabre-toothed shaggy hunter galloped down,
Drunk with the blood of she-goats from the hills.
His drumming hooves excited primal terror,
Regret and fascination: he was Death.

Soul heard, and trembled in the febrile glade
Where the grey elders slew the holy ram
And spilt its entrails to assuage
Their nomad fear.

      And there the soul found strength
To break the blurred delirious veils
Of silence and of pathos and of self;
And went with unavailing arms
To meet the drumming hooves, the winding horn,
The baying hounds of lust, the centaur's teeth,

And there gave witness with his blood
According to the word of God.

After Dunkirk

I have been silent a lifetime
As a stabbed man,
And stolid, showing nothing
As a refugee.
But inwardly I have wept.
The blood has flown inwardly into the spirit
Through the gaping wound of the world.
And only the little worm,
The small white tapeworm of the soul,
Lived on unknown within my blood.

But now I have this boon, to speak again,
I have no more desire to express
The old relationships, of love fulfilled
Or stultified, capacity for pain,
Nor to say gracefully all that the poets have said
Of one or other of the old compulsions.
For now the times are gathered for confession.

First, then, remember Faith
Haggard with thoughts that complicate
What statesmen's speeches try to simplify;
Horror of war, the ear half-catching
Rumours of rape in crumbling towns;
Love of mankind, impelling men
To murder and to mutilate; and then
Despair of man that nurtures self-contempt
And makes men toss their careless lives away,
While joy becomes an idiot's grin
Fixed in a shaving mirror in whose glass
The brittle systems of the world revolve.

And next, the rough immediate life of camp
And barracks where the phallic bugle rules
The regimented orchestra of love;
The subterfuges of democracy, the stench
Of breath in crowded tents, the grousing queues,

And bawdy songs incessantly resung
And dull relaxing in the dirty bar;
The difficult tolerance of all that is
Mere rigid brute routine; the odd
Sardonic scorn of desolate self-pity,
The pathetic contempt of the lonely for the crowd;
And, as the crystal slowly forms,
A growing self-detachment making man
Less home-sick, fearful, proud,
But less a man.
Beneath all this
The dark imagination that would pierce
Infinite night and reach the waiting arms
And soothe the guessed-at tears.

And then the final change. For discipline
Becomes a test of self; one learns to bear
Insult as quietly as if it were
A physical deformity. But hope
Has left the calm humanity that waits
In silence for the zero hour.
That first great ordeal over,
New resolution grows
In shell-shocked minds of frightened boys
To live again, within the heightened vision
Of life as they saw it in the hour of battle
When the worn and beautiful faces of the half-forgotten
Came softly round them with the holy power
To raise the wounded and the dying succour,
Making complete all that was misbegotten
Or clumsily abused or left neglected.

And as the burning town falls down the wake
And white waves spread their fans and day grows
bright,
Then sea and sky and wheeling gulls commingle
In the smiles of dying children and the joy
Of luckier babies playing in the cot.

From a Play

We are the little men grown huge with death.
Stolid in squads or grumbling on fatigues,
We held the honour of the regiment
And stifled our antipathies.
Stiff-backed and parrot-wise with pamphlet learning,
We officiated at the slaughter of the riverine peoples
In butcheries beyond the scope of our pamphlets.
We had certain authority for this;
Not ours, but Another's;
Our innocence remained with us.

Only one night, after the slaughter,
With the moon swaying across the river
And black-headed kittiwakes and oyster-catchers
Fishing the silver,
We stood in the shadows, waiting events in Europe,
Till some fantastic longing took us
With love for people of another world.

And we saw the light chaste school-girls of our boyhood
Singing upon the lake, and we remembered
Pied stonechats bobbing on the mountain rivers
Of an island in the first quarter.
And as we watched the sea-birds for an omen
We saw, moving along the line of hills,
The blond great-breasted goddess of pre-history
And in the stony glitter of her eyes
Divined our lonely destiny.

And no returning.

So we guarded our littleness with rifles
Till the foreign moon fell down by the sinister uplands
And daylight's green contusion tore the sky.
And now, on moonlit nights, we keep on seeing

Our faint familiar homeland haloed
In a rainbow of disease,

And all the good lads there that died. for luck.

Threnody for a Starry Night

I

White frost; intricate bare branches
Glittering with distant candles,
Glow-worms in the frozen hair
Of dead soldiers.
And on the broken arch of night
The Babylonian planets tell
The unromantic death of Keats.

The woman from the Egyptian rock-tomb
With the hawk's head and the chaste body
Has taken the frozen soldiers into her silence.
Her mood is pity; from the ice-bound poles
Of cynical Eternity she turns
Her head and weeps.
The dew is falling over Europe.
The diplomats wear astrakhan.
Beauty is hardness, ice.
All sons, all lovers
Death divides for ever, ever....
Only the lilies of the field
And this glittering tree endure
This silence ever.

II

The boy who climbed the creaking stairs
And floated on a couch at last
In that sordid attic found
His soul was rifled. Stumbling down,
Sobbing in the street he fled
Familiar things. His body
Suffers in khaki.
He disapproved Christ's chastity,
Chose warmth

Of loins, afraid to burn
Obedient martyr to a rigid creed;
Yet found
Christ crucified bequeathed
His agony to us.

III

Polish girls singing, in the wind's soughing:
We cannot go back. We dare not meet
The strangeness of our friendly street
Whose ruins lack
The clean porch, the shoe-scraper,
The Jewboy selling the evening paper,
The bow-window with the canary,
The house with a new baby,
The corner where our sweethearts waited
While we combed our hair.
We cannot return there.

By the mutilated smile,
By milk teeth smashed,
Love is outcast.
We choose the vast
Of dereliction which we fill
With grey affliction that shall spill
Out of our private parts like sawdust
From broken dolls.

IV

Socrates on the frozen lake
Sat awhile and heard, disconsolate,
The blind unnerving harmonies of fate.
And always in Shakespearean tragedy
The foils are poisoned that the good may die.

V

Now only beggars still go singing
And birds in forests.
We who are about
A mass rearming for mass-martyrdom
Are punctual and silent.

Where sweet eyes were
Now are hollow craters.
Love's torn head in lassitude
Lies on the pillow,
And sister Ophelia, over-worked,
Sings willow, green willow.

VI

Sweet Mother Church, beleaguered on the hill
Of hesitation half accepts
The amorous Protestant, but waits
A Balkan revelation. For the rest
She fits her soul to sacrifice
Countless humble peasant Christs.
And hobnailed soldiers smash the cracked mosaics
Of cross and crescent in the ravished fane.

VII

Lovers who among the grasses
Found the soul's sweet fern seed on their bodies,
Cross themselves now in superstition
Beneath the grinning and exalted gargoyles.

Perplexed with histories they wander
And seek in Palestinian lanes
The vast immortal Love of Other,

Till from the stone there grows a cross,
And dark conflicting shadows lengthening out
Like evening on the turbid centuries.

VIII

This stunted pine whose knotted roots
Suck water from the arid path,
Which drops its cones in season, breeding new,
More simply speaks the truth of it than we.
For we maintained
The state must wither in the end,
And soon forgot
That fire withers most
Armies as cities, frail as summer flowers.
Our passion scattered, yellow wasted leaves
Among the valleys suave with evening ease.

We were the daylight but we could not see.

Yet now at last, in shelter, tube and street,
Communal anguish banishes
Individual defeat.
Now in the crowded deadly places
Indifferent profiles have become
Beautiful tormented faces.

IX

The white brain crossing
The frontiers of darkness
To darkness and always
Darkness pursuing,
Finds asylum in a dreamless
Traumatic anguish where the planets
Stay at the stations where they gathered

In darkness of Creation;
Imperishable stars, the points of song,
Night's orchards budding in a lonely girl
Who sings in the throat of the thrush.

And in the dark the sensitive blind hands
Fashion the burning pitch of night
In lovely images of dawn.

The soldiers' frozen sightless eyes
End the mad feud. The worm is love.

Christmas Holiday

Big-uddered piebald cattle low
The shivering chestnut stallion dozes
The fat wife sighs in her chair
Her lap is filled with paper roses
The poacher sleeps in the goose-girl's arms
Incurious after so much eating
All human beings are replete.

But the cock upon the dunghill feels
God's needle quiver in his brain
And thrice he crows: and at the sound
The sober and the tipsy men
Jump out of bed with one accord
And start the war again.

The fat wife comfortably sleeping
Sighs and licks her lips and smiles

But the goose-girl is weeping.

Two Legends: for Greece

I

(Defeat)

When the raving tusked boar
Gored the sensual innocent,
The goddess heard it squeal and roar
In pride of blood on Venus' mount;
And winging like a wounded dove
Took flight from her disfigured love.

II

(Victory)

When Theseus in the labyrinth
Forgetting Beauty was aware
Of nothing but the minotaur's
Slavering jaws and bristling hair;

– The beast miraculously slain –

He stood indifferent in the whirl
Of a million careless faces.
And did some ignorant young girl
Unlatch the sandals off his feet
And with sweet oil anoint his pain
And lead him back to life again?

On a Bereaved Girl

She who yielded once
To the absolute of joy
Without the sanction of the Church
Is shrived now by the dying boy
Whose white absolving hands have laid
Silence upon her tongue and in her head.
She knows now in this grey
Negation of her life
That she can find no way
To lie beside him as his wife
And share his everlasting bed.

This further truth she knows –
Which Life must leave unsaid –
That the fled-away is eternal within her
And the devilry of the dead
Is also passionately flung away for ever
As she by hidden paths is led

By his deep silence summoned down
Through the sunken worlds of birth
Into the final grim delirium
Of the act of Death-on-Earth;
And deeper still, to where all action
Is sinless, sexless, and reverts
Into the slime of thought which rots away
The grafted skin and clinging cerements,
The little caves and meadows of the flesh,
And all the fond forgotten lineaments

And leaves the floating mesh,
The soul,
Some shape,
Unknown . . .

Peace

The wind blows
Through her eyes,
Snow is banked
In her whiter thighs,
The birds are frantic with
Her last distress,
And flutter and chatter over
Her nakedness.

And her blind
Eyes are prayers
Where she lies
By the boulders
The strong shoulders
Of the Earth
Who is kind
And will harvest
Her prayers
And abideth
His time.

Destroyed is the well
Of her magic,
But where she lies silent
And tragic the earth
Pallid in reverie
Stirs with the birth
Of the flowers, the white
And the red that she gives,

The tendrils and swarming of all
That still lives, *oh still lives!*

And she comes from the dead,
Smiling, without mystery,
Homeward slowly turning
Century by century.

And all the heart's deep yearning
In her Being is burning, burning.

Easter at Christmas

What dark and terrible shadow is swaying in the wind?

Beautiful are thy dwellings, Lord of Hosts,
The choir-boys in white go softly singing;
The world is full of pale frustrated ghosts.

Lovers cannot reach each other;
The stars are consumed by an insane fire;
The night is red and loud; the choir-boys
Sing softly ghostly vespers of desire.

What dark and terrible shadow is swaying in the wind?

An agitator and two thieves are swaying in the wind.

Post-Script: for Gweno

If I should go away,
Beloved, do not say
'He has forgotten me'.
For you abide,
A singing rib within my dreaming side;
You always stay.
And in the mad tormented valley
Where blood and hunger rally
And Death the wild beast is uncaught, untamed,
Our soul withstands the terror
And has its quiet honour
Among the glittering stars your voices named.

Poems in Love

Fever

I felt the universe with my fingers; and it was
     compounded of bone and sinew, like the naked
     loins of Theseus, the slayer, the young hero,

And of softness, like petals, like pools of water
     glimmering between pine roots and birches when
     the moon is ripe for harvest,

And of blood, like the roar of a torrent, a landslide,
     a battle, delirious weeping or the laughter of children.

But it was night; and the universe was grey like
     charred rafters, and like fungus pocked with
     red stars, like fever.
I took its stem and plucked the rain-swollen toadstool;
     and ate it, tasting its bitterness in my mouth.

Convulsed, I saw the stars reeling outside my window,
     the Sword flashing and the Plough wrecked in the branches;
And through the barred grating I clamoured for
     relief; for sunlight wrapped in an envelope, for
     a day's dole;

And I signed my name on God's register with quivering fingers.

Oh my love! Why did I dream this dream in my
     bed; feeling your nearness

And the panting of your belly and the gentle murmuring
     of your breath,

Only to wake to the loneliness of the deserted
     and the agony of silence

And the mockery of my desire's trembling mirage?
Oh my love!

               who like the sunlight
Can strike and blind and parch.

The Desperate

When the soul is mad
With foiled desire,
And whirls the flesh
In an arc of fire;

When the mind's a fever
And the grey brain drips,
And the virgin seeks
Polluted lips,

O man and woman
In that hour of need,
Fling wide the sluice,
Release the seed;

And Love, poor Love
Must bear the ache
Of lust grown holy
For the soul's sweet sake.

Mid-Winter

Old Dafydd, eyes like bloodhound's red with age,
Told me in passing, dropping his brushwood to say,
'The waves freeze as they fall. It is indeed
'Funny to hear that silence, 'tis indeed!"
And blew upon his blue and broken nails
And rubbed his mittened hands and shouldered up
The ice and earth encrusted twigs of beech
And said 'Good night. And mind in this cold spell
You do not loiter', and then lumbered on.

I took the path to the sea along the ruts
Whose crystals cracked and crunched beneath my boots.
The frost-bound mountains, tuned like tightened strings,
Quivered beneath the hawk's exalted dream.
The disused quarry, red with peat and iron,
Suspended frozen stalactites of moss.
The briars' vernal thrust
Writhed vainly in the icewomb of the soil,
And all the meadows screamed through sharp green tongues
Dumbly and blacklipped stretched upon the rack,
For the loosening laughter of rain and the runnels' race.
And I like the grass cried out
In the ice of your absence clutched
For the sun in the sunken night,
For a proof of your escape,
For your coming home.

And when I came to the shore I felt you pull
My heart as the passionate wave
Answered the moontug, leaped, and in high poise
Tense in a timeless curve contained itself,
Then broke, ah broke, and shattered and seethed all white
Up the green and purple pebble beach – the reach
Of desire that rushes white from the swirl of pain.
So my heart leaped high and ached for your coming again
As the earth for the longed-for, long awaited
Blessing of the rain.

At last the benediction, the soft release,
The bending of grass, the dripping from moss and leaf,
When I heard the fall of your sandal on the sand
And I felt your body breathing by my side,
When my heart like a grove of birds sang back again
Your coming, your home-returning, farer-forth,
To my charred and ashen hearth whose heap of sticks
Your nostril's breath rekindles, Cytherea,
Who stand so silent, hesitant, engrossed.
O warm your aching hands
At my soul's reviving flame,
And tell me, if you choose,
Of your troubled voyaging down
Through the chasms of time and pain,
Of the stress of the rocks on your soul,
And your soul's escape.

But your puckered forehead and distracted eyes
Tell of a madness too intense for word
Or kiss or loving pity to dispel.
Yet, having come to me,
Lie quietly, beloved, in my arms;
Let us forget
In the warmth of the flesh the dry and hidden bone,
In the curve of the wave its shattering on the stone,
And sleep within my breathing, sweetheart, sleep,
While the wood smoke curls through Dafydd's leaking thatch
And the river runs again with gladness to the sea.

Valediction

Through the trembling blue the golden porpoise plunged,
The white steeds whinnied and the wheels spun round;
Stars leaped from hoof and rim and burned to ash,
The madman's silver falchion clove the dusk.

The peasant penned his bullock in the croft
And hung its tackle on the wooden peg
And yawned and went indoors. The safe latch shut.

But I, who waited for the moon to break
Clear from the clutch of the thing I dreaded most,
Lay terrified amid the brooding gorse
And waited – till my young face wrinkled up,
My hands grew fungus fingers, and my legs
Became two lopped logs rotting in the moss.
My heart ceased pulsing and my earth-stopped mouth
Slavered no more for Love or Food or Fear
Or You for whom my heart once paid too dear.

A Separation

She:

I died into his eyes
His hands refashioned me
His lips reshaped my lips.

The dead moon calls the sea
But the waves fall and break;
Their fall and break is a gesture
Of faith and of failure.

He:

The heart lies on its side
And aches unbearably;
The heart is a burden to the hands
Making them also ache.

Hands can forget

But what of the heart's pain
Seeking in hollows of Night
What the hands have slain?

War Wedding

I

The Vigil: He lies awake in the barrack room, fearful she will not come

The vulture stabs his beak into the sun.
The light falls bleeding from those beating wings.
The heat is taken in that ruthless heart.
The withered moon intones *She will not come.*

And if you will not come, then stuff
My wasted hours in a sack,
Cast off the threadbare day from my stale eyes,
And like a hawthorn fling your beauty
On the shambles of my love.

Into the gutters of darkness I bleed and bleed.
The moon has placed white pennies on my eyes.
The wounded beast beneath my lids
Hunched in a cave of broken myths
Among the groping outworn gods,
Strives for a straighter heaven
Than any the laughing sun affords.

And here the hiatus falls, the stammer,
The black-lipped wound that mouths oblivion;
Here children scream and blood is shed in vain
In a dark eclipse where the shadowy mistral blinds
Our daunted eyes and touches us to dust.

Here, on this chasm where the stars
Are splashed in powder in the reeling depths,
I tremble in nightmares of silence, calling your name.

II

The Vigil: She tarries, far-off, in a strange anguish

Salted and pierced sucked-in side
Of a martyr ripped to sea-weed shreds,
Your fanged blue tongue and bulging eyes
Remain as witness of your broken gesture.

They wanted only to break your gesture.
But all your gentle seed they took
And all your manly symmetry,
The soft ways of your speech
And all your laughter.

All life was active in your gesture.
But I refused you, threw you farther
Than heart's reach, nerves' tether....
Oh! Had I only slid my nails
Into your gaping cicatrice
And sucked you with my lips' leech-kisses
And been your pagan lover,
I would not shudder now the farmyard wakens
And cockcrow rips the lie out of my brain.

III

She comes to him in the night

But she is wise and waits until I sleep.
She will not touch the blindness from my eyes
Nor stroke the hair of silence on my loins
Nor bare her wistful breasts.
For first I must encounter
My dreaming German soldier.

And when my body falls away
Will come my useless saviour.

Ah! but I feel her gesture shiver
As she beckons in infinite space;
In the void of heaven and hell
She starts the shrivelled heart
Of the panting moon awake.
And I rise from the restless armies
That cough like huddled sheep.
I lay the soiled red tourniquet aside,
She lies within my sleep.
Her golden hair is freed
About me and the thirsty stars
Are shaken from the mantling tree
And light the dark bruised seed.
The unborn children are singing
As we sail softly homing.

IV

He gives her Botticelli's Birth of Venus as a Wedding Gift

Sweet Florentine, sea-spawned
Medusa of the jetty where
The coast wise traders ply,
When the wind lifts the plaited rays
Of your serpentine gold hair
The wind is caught and sung
In the vortex of heaven.
Whorled periwinkle, breathless wave
Kissing the sighing pebble-green,
Deep rock-pools' trembling lucency
Through which the sunburnt Tyrian dives
For the pearl in its dark yolk,
Your sad and wistful smile is glad

To know the Tyrian sleeps at last
In the sea-anemone that sways
Beneath the surface of the tide
And feels its silken veins.

V

The Marriage Bed

Draw a green cedar over the peeping sky,
Latch the grey sash across the glancing sea,
Close the dark door and lie within the rose,
Beloved, lie with me.

My heavy boots stand sentinel against
This hired bedroom underneath the eaves,
Where Beauty slips the green leash of her Spring
And flowers blossom from a ring of leaves.

And in her white magnetic fields
My tense prismatic fingers move
In patterns of attraction and release;
The parallels tend unswervingly
Towards the pole of peace.

The fragile universe of self
In all its fine integrity
Becomes a cosmic curve, a thrust
Of natural fertility;
And Gods who shivered in the dust
Have found their lost divinity.

And if to-night it chance we weep,
None shall know of our distress;
We are the bread and wine who share the feast;
The elements are in our nakedness.

Black cedar, hide the peeping day;
Sun, lie awhile beneath the sea;
And rose, within your velvet heart
Keep her, and me.

VI

She wakes early, while he still sleeps

Conflicting rumours of the swaying fight
Resolve in the agitation of pigeons,
Fantails flutter in the callous light
That calls him from me into battle.

My lover is a soldier,
He brought me all his trouble;
I thought my heart would break
That bitter joy to slake.

But now he lies like honeysuckle
His wounded hands a blessing on my breasts.

And softly the night still slants in silver
On the four white towers gliding down-river.

VII

They part at daybreak, returning their inevitable ways

Cradled in the smiling moon,
The tiny child of passion cries
With griping pains, then suddenly
Lies happy in the island of a smile.

Eagles of suffering hang across the moon,
Their shadows fall upon the smiling child,
The terrible black eagles that hover
In ceaseless vigil, the world over.

Enter the smile of the child, Jehovah,
O God of battle, take its mother
And in my stead be Thou her pagan lover.

Wanting a miracle by day and night,
Gripped in the boneless tentacles of grief,
The miracle I seek is peace.

She said I made her fertile with a smile.
But now the reaper shaves his head
And goes to harvest with the dead
Far from the pastures of his fond desire
While War sets all her golden fields afire.

VIII

She remains

The four white towers slowly glide
In calm communion with the tide.

The city changes hands by day and night,
A whore for whom the drunkards fight.

Where Love surrenders in that brawl
Their names are scrawled in blood along the wall.

Songs

Miniature on a Book of Hours

The grass so green, the sky so blue,
And under a flowering pear-tree white
Two lovers locked in deep delight,
The green, the blue, the whole day through;
While the serpent basks in the gentle sun
And waits till the pretty play is done.

Creavisti, Domine; Gaudeamus Igitur.

The Dancer

'He's in his grave and on his head
I dance,' the lovely dancer said,
'My feet like fireflies illume
The choking blackness of his tomb.'

'Had he not died we would have wed,
And still I'd dance,' the dancer said,
'To keep the creeping sterile doom
Out of the darkness of my womb.'

'Our love was always ringed with dread
Of death,' the lovely dancer said,
'And so I danced for his delight
And scorched the blackened core of night
With passion bright,' the dancer said –

'And now I dance to earn my bread.'

Songs for the Night

I

Stars seem gilded nipples
Of the Night's vast throbbing breasts,
Softly disclosing themselves at the fall of dark....
Or warriors' nodding crests
The moon-mad darkness ripples,
Making the terrified watchdogs rattle their chains and bark.

II

Black dog barking at the moon,
Beauty fallen in a swoon;
White snow melts where it is red,
Beauty's face is pinched with dread;
Curtains fall across the night,
But memory imprisons sight;

And always, ringing in the ear,
The tramp of feet, the scream of fear.

III

Under each starry leafless tree
Lovers lie in ecstasy,
While over every trembling thing
Orion's sword hangs glittering.

Songs of Sleep

I

With joy my heart
Is singing
Silently;
Fearful to start
Again my soul
To weeping.

For by my joy I know
My soul
Is sleeping.

II

Grief in the dusk lulled Joy to sleep
And gently brushed the tears from off his lashes,
And grey-eyed watched the whitening crumbling ashes
Of the day's fire,
Love's pyre.

Autumn, 1939

The beech boles whiten in the swollen stream;
Their red leaves, shaken from the creaking boughs,
Float down the flooded meadow, half in dream
Seen in a mirror cracked by broken vows,
Water-logged, slower, deeper, swirling down
Between the indifferent hills who also saw
Old jaundiced knights jog listlessly to town
To fight for love in some unreal war.

Black leaves are piled against the roaring weir;
Dark closes round the manor and the hut;
The dead knight moulders on his rotting bier,
And one by one the warped old casements shut.

The Encounter

She said 'I came a weary way
By camel through the dead salt sea;
Oh Solomon, from Sheba
I came to visit thee.'

He watched the moonstone rise and fall
On the woman's milk-white breast;
And his soul was like the silken shift
Through which her nipples pressed.

Royalty fell off with its robes,
Wisdom lay dumb with lust;
The Ancient Leveller there laid
Zion and Sheba in the dust.

On Old Themes

The Captivity

I

They have clippped the wings of my doves, my messengers
    of delight,
And they in whom I have delighted have been shackled
    with chains.
They are sent to toil in the claypits, they are become quarriers
    of stones:
The harp and the lute have been taken from their hands,
They have forgotten their delight.

O remembrances curdle the milk in my breasts,
And my breath is sour to recall my joy,
For I also am in bondage in the land of Pharaoh.

II

The fishes inhabit the deep rock crannies, the worm the dry
    wood, the badger the darkness of earth.
There are they content, for there is their home.

But my content lies not in the land of Pharaoh,
And my soul is sick with love amid the laughter of the land.

III

Pharaoh has seen me in the hovels of Israel;
My beauty has burned in his veins, he has said
'Toads shall not dwell in the cup of the lily,
Nor she in the hovels of Israel.'

His artisans made me a palace of marble,
The ceilings they builded of beaten gold,
The walls they made lovely with lapis and amethyst
Chalcedony sardonyx amber and jade.
The workmen of Pharaoh hewed cedars of Lebanon
And bound them in rafts and sailed them to Nile.
My bed they did hew of sweet cedars of Lebanon.

O Lebanon! Pharaoh shall share not my bed.

IV

The swallows are nesting in the hovels of Israel,
But the windows of my palace are dim with rain, and my
        eyes see not for their tears.
The echoes of my longing fall faint in the silence
Of the high vaulted arch, of the ceilings of beaten gold.
In the infinite corridors of my habitation my longing is lost;
Polluted with longing are my channels of blood,
Down which my heart floats, ah! white swan.

And shall I become a pearl of Pharaoh, and my palace a
        show-thing for his people?
Or shall the scoffers say one to the other
'The daughter of Israel is sick of self-love' and then,
        'She is dead of her pride'?
Yet is my soul a fly that feeds on garbage?
And shall my body wax with the lust of Pharaoh?

My nostrils are filled with the dust of desire,
My bare feet bleed on the shards of despair,
In the labyrinth of remembrance my longing is lost.

V

At dusk in my garden the flowers are waiting,
Like virgins who linger by the house of their love,
Whose hearts in the darkness are saying and saying
'If my beloved will come to the street in the darkness, his
      heart shall not lack nor his loins want their desire.'
And ever they linger; for how shall the heart's timid whisper
      be heard?
But my ears have heard the scythe of Pharaoh at harvest
      in the fields of Israel.
He has garnered the corn and the poppies has he mown
      down.
How then shall I joy in the flowers of Pharaoh?
And how shall I lie in his bed?

VI

The gates of my palace are opened wide
And the air is rank with the lust of Pharaoh.
His naked feet sound in the halls of my palace,
He lighteth his way to my room with a torch.

Yet will I be still.
In the waters of my body he shall satisfy his thirst.
For the gates of my palace are opened wide
And my doves have flown home from the land of Pharaoh.

My heart is escaped in its night.

Poems from the Chinese

1

Mine Host

Linger not in my library,
If you seek in it wisdom, not pleasure.
Before you turn to my bookshelves, listen.
Green ivy fingers tap the window,
Calling the eyes to the slope of orchard.
My son is fishing in the pond,
And beyond,
The grass is blanched as for a wedding,
Under the orchard trees, with idle blossom.
My library door adjoins the orchard –
An you wisely seek for pleasure,
It will let you pass.

2

The Civil Servant

In cities is always the expectation
To glimpse an inner court through some dark doorway,
Where nods with sun and the sound of doves
A wrinkled old woman in black silk sitting
Under the fig.
And in the country are intenser pleasures,
In all seasons, fingers and eyes rejoicing.
And seldom does my heart hold this sharp sorrow,
Of knowing that these joys are only mine,
Attending consummation with no woman.
Blue mists float on the stream – Warmer my fire
And the usual chair.
                    I must beware
Not to disturb the lovers by the sallow,
Returning through the meadow.

3

The Country Gentleman

I, who have the gift of almost seeing
A goblin in wood fires;
I, to whom the frost is an embalming
Of butterflies' wings;
I, who can wait in the sedge the kingfisher's flight
And count the expectance worth the not seeing –
I find it truly unfortunate
That my wife should be unhappily barren
And my crop withered with blight.
It was not essential that either of these things should fall,
And break my communing.

4

The Merchant's Wife

My son would not have been born,
To fetch me lotus for my bosom,
To gladden my heart and my house,
Had I not often smiled upon his father.
I count it a blessing that my son was born, and know
That wisdom is in smiling.

5

The Poet

Five slender birches grouped in peace,
Five silver boles at the end of the wood, lifting a green head.
The thunder breaks across them in the pent-up sky.
And I, uncomfortably feeling the sky's need,
Cannot sense the slenderness of the five birches.

Then the liberation of rain on the parched leaves,
On the cracked thunder lips,
On the scorched breath of lightning,
– Ceasing –
and leaving to me the five birches.

The Odyssey

When we sailed homewards burning embers
Fell softly hissing round us in the harbour;
The burning towers thundered valedictions,
The lurid waters gave no homeward welcome;
And shamefully we fled away from Troy.

We fared uncertain of our end, bewaring
Our heart's spasmodic hope or too close thinking
On Ithaca's fast harbour where the galleys
Rode side by side between the thrusting headlands,
Its olive groves and women in the vineyards.
We had a spate of wenching inside Troy.

Rocks and inhospitable headlands and the sea,
The vain reiteration of our longing,
The silences, the long morose inbrooding
Exercised on us all a strange indifference,
While all the time our craft sailed like a bloodclot
The intricate sea-veins and sought the brain
Where even the fanciful lotus would fail to still our pain.
We left oblivion far behind us, in the reeking courts of Troy.

Mazed in the mesh of islands we forgot
The future; we imagined what had passed.
We lost cognition of reality amidst
The perpetual circling and swirl of the sea-birds,
The ball of fire, the singing from the island,
The flocking seals upon the black-fanged rocks,
The soft white clashing of the gulf streams,
The panting nymphs, the centaurs on the cliff-tops,
The slow approach of winter after winter,
The haggard mornings when we thought of Troy.

In Cyclops' cavern and in witch's pigsty
Deeper than fear or hate we knew the ache
For simpler things, the smart of sunburnt shoulder,
The dip of oars, the joke and all its laughter,

The times we traded peacefully with Troy.
But Circe and Calypso kept our master
And everywhere he feasted long and bragged
More than was decent of his ancient exploits.

What did he fear to find at the end of the voyage?

His wife grown ugly, withered hands and lips
Mumbling a garbled story of his youth?
Or joy and ripeness in the flowing acres
And merry children – by another man?
Did he fear LIFE?

                He drank too much and boasted
Too much about his ancient violence.
His eyes were mad each time he talked of Troy.

But still we sailed, like ugly gods enduring
The day-spring glittering with beauty,
And one of us kept notching up the moons
Along the rotting gunwale; still we kept
A fitful knowledge of ourselves; we wove
Into the pattern of our nervous thoughts
A vague confusing longing for the fields,
Homesteads and wives and children grown to manhood,
The pastoral life, the common satisfaction
Forfeited when we answered wrong with wrong.

And still at sunset we beheld the bastions
And burning towers of the lovely city
Immortalized by its destruction.
We knew that vision of a ruined age
To be the shape our minds and deeds had fashioned,
And we ourselves to be a wretched omen

Tossed in the tides and never making landfall,
A dying race whose doom it was to live.

And what blind man, singing of ruined Troy,
Will understand and pity her destroyers?

And what old mangy dog will know us when we come
To Ithaca, and shiver with delight?

The Swan's Way

I changed myself into a swan
To satisfy my lechery,
And folded with my milk-white wings
Leda in sweet ecstasy.

And then I saw her childish eyes
Grow lunatic with shame
As one the horsey farm lads force
To play their cowshed game.

Her horror pierced my godhead through.
I fled, my lust forespent.
'Oh hearken!' all the mortals cried,
'A dying swan's lament!'

Horace at Twenty

The nightingales sing, Lalage,
Thrilling the night's black soul,
But I lie alone, alone, Lalage;
The darkness has made me whole.

Why so haggard, Lalage?
Do your lonely raptures cloy?
I thought you were too selfish, Lalage,
To mourn a broken boy.

The wan night sickens, Lalage,
Wash your white cheeks and go.
Everything has its limits, Lalage –
'Twas you that told me so.

And Other Poems

The Madman

I

The shattered crystal of his mind
Flashes its dangerous splinters in the sun.
His eyes conceal behind their jagged smile
The madness of his helplessness.
His laughter has the sound of weeping.

II

The sensual mind in the wreaths of wine
Deflowers with its touch the tangible,
But cannot save the bloom, the dust, the pollen,
The glow of beauty, its soft immanence.
The madman has that wonder in his eyes.

He knows life is a beautiful girl who loves no one
Yet makes the mirrors glitter and men mad.
And he has lived a lifetime with a virgin,
Peacefully, like Joseph of Nazareth.
His weeping has the sound of laughter.

III

He sees the dawn expanding from a seashell
In delicate whorls of coloured music
Developing through countless variations
Of branches and skylines and streams winding,
Through perfect mutations of mountain and cloud and cattle,
Tree, bush and bird, the single pebble
Washed a smooth oval, grain and blossom

Multiplied till, his mind dissolved in vastness,
He takes the breeze in all his towering canvas
And sails sublimely on without a compass.

IV

Exultantly he drives his screaming pinnace
Through the clashing ocean of love.
His dripping keel cleaves deep. And snow-white birds
Wheel round and round his prow.

Yet all the storm is but a lover's gesture,
The glittering constellations are his seed,
His mast, a rose tree softly lapped in leaf,
Sucks up the salt sap of his timeless grief.

V

His mind is an inarticulated question.
The universe evolves its slow and painful answer.

Meanwhile the darkness breaks and forms again
Round the fiendish accusing fingers of his dreams,
The incantations of silence, God's terrible silence,
And the maddening ultimate beauty of the dreamed
          angelic faces.

The Mountain over Aberdare

From this high quarried ledge I see
The place for which the Quakers once
Collected clothes, my fathers' home,
Our stubborn bankrupt village sprawled
In jaded dusk beneath its nameless hills;
The drab streets strung across the cwm,
Derelict workings, tips of slag
The gospellers and gamblers use
And children scrutting for the coal
That winter dole cannot purvey;
Allotments where the collier digs
While engines hack the coal within his brain;
Grey Hebron in a rigid cramp,
White cheap-jack cinema, the church
Stretched like a sow beside the stream;
And mourners in their Sunday best
Holding a tiny funeral, singing hymns
That drift insidious as the rain
Which rises from the steaming fields
And swathes about the skyline crags
Till all the upland gorse is drenched
And all the creaking mountain gates
Drip brittle tears of crystal peace;
And in a curtained parlour women hug
Huge grief, and anger against God.

But now the dusk, more charitable than Quakers,
Veils the cracked cottages with drifting may
And rubs the hard day off the slate.
The colliers squatting on the ashtip
Listen to one who holds them still with tales,
While that white frock that floats down the dark alley
Looks just like Christ; and in the lane
The clink of coins among the gamblers
Suggests the thirty pieces of silver.

I watch the clouded years
Rune the rough foreheads of these moody hills,
This wet evening, in a lost age.

The Rhondda

Hum of shaft-wheel, whirr and clamour
Of steel hammers overbeat, din down
Water-hag's slander. Greasy Rhondda
River throws about the boulders
Veils of scum to mark the ancient
Degraded union of stone and water.

Unwashed colliers by the river
Gamble for luck the pavements hide.
Kids float tins down dirty rapids.
Coal-dust rings the scruffy willows.
Circe is a drab.
She gives men what they know.
Daily to her pitch-black shaft
Her whirring wheels suck husbands out of sleep.
She for her profit takes their hands and eyes.

But the fat flabby-breasted wives
Have grown accustomed to her ways.
They scrub, make tea, peel the potatoes
Without counting the days.

Destruction

This is the street I inhabit.
Where my bread is earned my body must stay.
This village sinks drearily deeper
In its sullen hacked-out valley
And my soul flies ever more rarely
To the eyries among these Welsh mountains.

Massive above the dismantled pitshaft
The eight-arched viaduct clamps the sky with stone.
Across the high-flung bridge a goods train rumbles,
Its clanking wagons make my fixed rails rock,
And the smoke from its engine blows higher than my desire;
Its furnace glowers in my vast grey sky.

Under this viaduct of my soul
The poisoned river makes its dirty bed,
Wherein a girl lies dreaming, diffusing attar of roses.
And I in bitterness wonder
Why love's silk thread should snap,
Though the hands be never so gentle;
And why a destructive impulse should ruin a poem,
Like a schoolboy's sling that slays a swallow flashing
Under the viaduct's arch to the inaccessible eaves.

And now the impersonal drone of death
Trembles the throbbing night, the bombers swoop,
The sky is ripped like sacking with a scream.
The viaduct no longer spans the stream.

But my love knows nothing of that grim destruction,
For the night was about her, blinding her when she crossed it,
And the train that took her roaring towards the dayspring
Is rocking her through the dawn down empty sidings
Between dark tenements in the neutral city
To the street she must inhabit.

Lines on a Young Girl

To see the intolerant toss of her silken head,
Her childish sulking by the rainsoaked window;
Her small breasts' self-assertion, – nipples pressed

Against the closely moulded, dreamed-of dress, –
The troubled flowering of her restless body
Chafing within this chaste much-mothered home,
Is to set a desperate value upon her presence
Here, in this kitchen, drying her hair by the fire
Before her footsteps take her where in daydream
Her drifting eyes like butterflies now wander
Among the dockyards of red roving men.

Her adolescence like an outgrown dress
She'll fiercely cast off for her protean lover
Who'll burn her whiteness, set her flesh on fire:
And for her soul, its childhood-deep desire,
She'll still that yearning in the stony city
When young boys tap the well-spring of her pity.

Atropos to Ophelia

(Atropos to Ophelia, in the palace garden playing:)

Your feigned indifference hardly hides your love
For young prince Hamlet who paces the arbour of roses.
And you whose forehead is unfurrowed with fore-
     knowledge
May play awhile with him in whose dark mind
Huge tortured thoughts lie fallow.

And yet you may not see
If he be Life or Death, or Good or Evil;
Nor can your heart distinguish Joy from Pain.
And when he goes, the child of your desire
Shall be a visitation projected but not made;
His birth without rejoicing,
No sorrow at his death;
His voice shall be the waiting for a word unspoken,
His life a highroad empty of footsteps;
His birth and his death shall be one thing, and then
     no thing,
The womb and the coffin shall be one place, and then
     no place.

But soft! He beckons. And your modest smile
Is ignorant as sunlight on his limbs.
This is your life, this welcome of the sun.
Give of your warmth, then, to the sable stranger.

The Humanist

Crivelli, dead four hundred years and more,
Loved gardening best of all and spent his day
Gainlessly mooning through the high-piled store
Of country produce – artichoke and bay,
Lentils and lemons – haggling with the folk,
Then showing his empty pockets as a joke

Till 'Fie on such delights,' his aching guts did crow
Like starving cockerels, 'Use your latent gift
For draughtmanship and subtly mixing paints.'

The Church paid well, and he, unused to thrift,
Made his toil lighter, as his paintings show,
By strewing marrows carefully about the feet of saints.

The East

'If passion and grief and pain and hurt
Are but the anchorite's hair-shirt,
Can such a torment of refining
Be aimless wholly, undesigning?

Must
Such aching
Go to making
Dust?'

Whispered the wind in the olive tree
In the garden of Gethsemane.

Ha! Ha! Among the Trumpets
Poems in Transit

Part One: England

Dawn on the East Coast

From Orford Ness to Shingle Street
The grey disturbance spreads
Washing the icy seas on Deben Head.

Cock pheasants scratch the frozen fields,
Gulls lift thin horny legs and step
Fastidiously among the rusted mines.

The soldier leaning on the sandbagged wall
Hears in the combers' curling rush and crash
His single self-centred monotonous wish;

And time is a froth of such transparency
His drowning eyes see what they wish to see;
A girl laying his table with a white cloth.

* * * * *

The light assails him from a flank,
Two carbons touching in his brain
Crumple the cellophane lanterns of his dream.

And then the day, grown feminine and kind,
Stoops with the gulfing motion of the tide
And pours his ashes in a tiny urn.
From Orford Ness to Shingle Street
The grey disturbance lifts its head
And one by one, reluctantly,
The living come back slowly from the dead.

Corfe Castle

Framed in a jagged window of grey stones
These wooded pastures have a dream-like air.
You thrill with disbelief
To see the cattle move in a green field.

Grey Purbeck houses by the sun deceived
Sleep with the easy conscience of the old;
The swathes are sweet on slopes new harvested;
Householders prune their gardens, count the slugs;
The beanrows flicker flowers red as flames.

Those to whom life is a picture card
Get their cheap thrill where here the centuries stand
A thrusting mass transfigured by the sun
Reeling above the streets and crowing farms.
The rooks and skylarks are okay for sound,
The toppling bastions innocent with stock.

Love grows impulsive here: the best forget;
The failures of the earth will try again.
She would go back to him if he but asked.
The tawny thrush is silent; when he sings
His silence is fulfilled. Who wants to talk
As trippers do? Yet, love,
Before we go be simple as this grass.
Lie rustling for this last time in my arms.
Quicken the dying island with your breath.

Compassion

She in the hurling night
With lucid simple hands
Stroked away his fright
Loosed his bloodsoaked bands

And seriously aware
Of the terror she caressed
Drew his matted hair
Gladly to her breast.

And he who babbled Death
Shivered and grew still
In the meadows of her breath
Restoring his dark will.

Nor did she ever stir
In the storm's calm centre
To feel the tail, hooves, fur
Of the god-faced centaur.

A Welsh Night

Fine flame of silver birches flickers
Along the coal-tipped misty slopes
Of old Garth mountain who tonight
Lies grey as a sermon of patience
For the threadbare congregations of the anxious.
Huddled in black-out rows the streets
Hoard the hand-pressed human warmth
Of families round a soap-scrubbed table;
Munition girls with yellow hands
Clicking bone needles over khaki scarves,
Schoolboys' painful numerals in a book,
A mother's chilblained fingers soft
Upon the bald head of a suckling child,
But no man in the house to clean the grate
Or bolt the outside door or share the night.
Yet everywhere through cracks of light
Faint strokes of thoughtfulness feel out
Into the throbbing night's malevolence,
And turn its hurt to gentler ways.

Hearing the clock strike midnight by the river
This village buried deeper than the corn
Bows its blind head beneath the angelic planes,
And cherishing all known and suffered harm
It wears the darkness like a shroud or shawl.

Westminster Abbey

Discoloured lights slant from the high rose window
Upon the sightseers and the faithful
And those who shelter from the rain this Sunday.
The clergy in their starched white surplices
Send prayers like pigeons circling overhead
Seeking the ghostly hands that give them bread.

The togaed statesmen on their scribbled plinths
Stand in dull poses, dusty as their fame
Crammed in the chapter of a schoolboy's book;
Their eyes have lost their shrewd and fallible look.

Kneeling by Gladstone is a girl who sobs.
Something profounder than the litany
Moves in the dark beneath the restless steps
Of this pale swirl of human flux.
Soft fingers touch the worn marmoreal stone.
The pale girl reaches out for what has gone.

The thin responsions falter in the air.
Only the restless footsteps hurry on,
Escaping that which was in the beginning,
Is now, and ever shall be.

                              – See, the girl
Adjusts her fashionable veil.
The vergers clack their keys, the soldiers go,
The white procession shuffles out of sight.
The incubus is shifted to the stars,
The flux is spun and drifted through the night,
And no one stays within that holy shell
To know if that which IS be good or ill.

Jason and Medea

The night appeared to authorise it.
The snakes were curling in her tallow hair,
And he stood in the weak and fascinating
Pallour of singing sexes, debonair,
Knowing her hungry glance, her cool attraction,
The cheap and placid aroma of her smile.
Tomorrow was a carton of abstraction,
A little debt he always could defer.
And in a nest of snakes he courted her.

Infantry

By day these men ask nothing, and obey;
They eat their bread behind a heap of stones;
Hardship and violence grow an easy way,
Winter is like a girl within their bones.

They learn the gambits of the soul,
Think lightly of the themes of life and death,
All mortal anguish shrunk into an ache
Too nagging to be worth the catch of breath.

Sharing Life's iron rations, marching light,
Enduring to the end the early cold,
The emptiness of noon, the void of night
In whose black market they are bought and sold;
They take their silent stations for the fight.
Rum's holy unction makes the dubious bold.

Song

I lay in sheets of softest linen
Sleepless and my lover spoke
The word of Death within her sleep
And snuggled closer and awoke
And wrapped me in her snowwhite cloak,

And clasped me in exhausted arms
And swore I should not go again.
Her lips were writhing like a moth
Burnt in the steady lamp of pain.
But I was young and fain.

I heard the daylight wind its horn,
I saw the cloudy horsemen ride.
But my beloved lacked the strength
To keep me by her side
And I went forth in pride.

I clasped the burning sun all day,
The cold moon bled me white;
Then all things ended suddenly.
I saw the world take flight
And glitter in the starry night.

Encirclement

Wrapped in the night's diseases,
Haunted by streetwalking fancies
Of Coty and hunchbacks and sequins,
In the nameless dugouts and basements
Of Everyman's darkness,
I seek in the distant footfalls
The elusive answer of love,
Till deeper than any appearance
Or any one man's failure,
The shrivelled roots touch water.

And on this abandoned frontier
Where many visions falter
And youth and health are taken
Without complaint or reason,
I strive with the heart's blind strength
To reach the mild and patient place
Where the lamplit room awaits a stranger
And suffering has sanctified your face.

Song

Oh journeyman, Oh journeyman,
Before this endless belt began
Its cruel revolutions, you and she
Naked in Eden shook the apple tree.

Oh soldier lad, Oh soldier lad,
Before the soul of things turned bad,
She offered you so modestly
A shining apple from the tree.

Oh lonely wife, Oh lonely wife,
Before your lover left this life
He took you in his gentle arms.
How trivial then were Life's alarms.

And though Death taps down every street
Familiar as the postman on his beat,
Remember this, Remember this
That Life has trembled in a kiss
From Genesis to Genesis,

And what's transfigured will live on
Long after Death has come and gone.

The Crucifixion

From the first he would not avoid it.
He knew they would stone and defile him, and looked
      to it calmly,
Riding to meet it serenely across the palm leaves, –
Processions in the East being near to bloodshed, –
Foreseeing a time when the body and all its injunctions
And *life* and *people* and all their persistent demands
Would desist, and they'd leave a policeman
Outside his door or his tomb to keep all in order
While he lay in supremest consummate passion
Passively passionate, suffering suffering only.

And this surrender of self to a greater statement
Has been desired by many more humble than he.
But when it came, was it other than he had imagined?
Breaking his Self up, convulsing his Father in pain?
His will prevented by every throbbing stigma,
The pangs that puffed and strained his stomach wall,
The utter weariness that bowed his head,
Taught him perhaps that more hung on the presence
Of all the natural preoccupations,
Duties, emotions, daily obligations
Affections and responses than he'd guessed.
They'd grown a burden to him, but as a mother
Is burdened by her child's head when her breasts
Are thin and milkless; he knew this awful hanging
Obscene with urine, sagging on a limb,
Was not the End of life, and improved nothing.

Sacco Writes to his Son

I did not want to die. I wanted you,
You and your sister Inez and your mother.
Reject this death, my Dante, seek out Life,
Yet not the death-in-life that most men live.
My body aches... I think I hear you weep.
You must not weep. Tears are a waste of strength.
Seven years your mother wept, not as your mother,
But as my wife. So make her more your mother.
Take her the ways I know she can escape
From the poor soulness that so wearies her.
Take her into the country every Sunday,
Ask her the name of such and such a plant,
Gather a basket each of herbs and flowers,
Ask her to find the robin where he nests,
She will be happy then. Tears do no damage
That spring from gladness, though they scald the throat.
Go patiently about it. Not too much
Just yet, Dante, good boy. You'll know.

And for yourself, remember in the play
Of happiness you must not act alone.
The joy is in the sharing of the feast.
Also be like a man in how you greet
The suffering that makes your young face thin.
Be not perturbed if you are called to fight.
Only a fool thinks life was made his way,
A fool or the daughter of a wealthy house.
Husband yourself, but never stale your mind
With prudence or with doubting. I could wish
You saw my body slipping from the chair
Tomorrow. You'd remember that, my son,
And would not weigh the cost of our struggle
Against the product as a poor wife does.
But I'll not break your sleep with such a nightmare.
You looked so happy when you lay asleep...

But I have neither strength nor room for all
These thoughts. One single thought's enough
To fill immensity. I drop my pen...

I hope this letter finds you in good health,
My son, my comrade. Will you give my love
To Inez and your mother and my friends.
Bartolo also sends his greetings to you.
I would have written better and more simple
Except my head spins like a dancing top
And my hand trembles . . . I am Oh, so weak . . .

Goodbye

So we must say Goodbye, my darling,
And go, as lovers go, for ever;
Tonight remains, to pack and fix on labels
And make an end of lying down together.

I put a final shilling in the gas,
And watch you slip your dress below your knees
And lie so still I hear your rustling comb
Modulate the autumn in the trees.

And all the countless things I shall remember
Lay mummy-cloths of silence round my head;
I fill the carafe with a drink of water;
You say 'We paid a guinea for this bed,'

And then, 'We'll leave some gas, a little warmth
For the next resident, and these dry flowers,'
And turn your face away, afraid to speak
The big word, that Eternity is ours.

Your kisses close my eyes and yet you stare
As though God struck a child with nameless fears;
Perhaps the water glitters and discloses
Time's chalice and its limpid useless tears.

Everything we renounce except our selves;
Selfishness is the last of all to go;
Our sighs are exhalations of the earth,
Our footprints leave a track across the snow.

We made the universe to be our home,
Our nostrils took the wind to be our breath,
Our hearts are massive towers of delight,
We stride across the seven seas of death.

Yet when all's done you'll keep the emerald
I placed upon your finger in the street;
And I will keep the patches that you sewed
On my old battledress tonight, my sweet.

Part Two: The Voyage

The Departure

Eyes closed, half waking, that first morning
He felt the curved grey bows enclose him,
The voyage beginning, the oceans giving way
To the thrust of steel, the pulse and beat
Of the engines that even now were revolving,
Revolving, rotating, throbbing along his brain
Rattling the hurried carpentry of his bunk,
Setting an unknown bearing into space.

He never thought that he might doubt or fear
Or lose himself or kill an honest man
Or die in some street outrage. Always there
Beneath the exertion and the novelty
Would be the deep sad rhythm of the process
Of the created thing awaking to the sound of the engine.

And he remembered all that was prevented,
How she came with him to the barrier
And knowing she could come no further
Turned back on the edge of his sleep,
Vexed, fumbling in her handbag,
Giving the world a dab of rouge and powder,
A toss of head, a passing hatred,
Going in all these trivial things, yet proudly;
Knowing more deeply than he the threat of his voyage,
With all a living woman's fear of death.

He heard the seagulls crying round the porthole
And in his sleepy trouble he knew the chafing
Of nettles her hands would be weaving into a garment
To turn her white-winged lover back to man,
A man released from the weary fluctuations
Of time and distance, forgetfulness and dying.

And then he woke unrested from his longing,
And locked himself and hurried to off-load
Boxes of ammunition from the wagons
And send them swaying from the groaning derricks
Deep into the unrefusing ship.

On Embarkation

I

Consider this silent disciplined assembly
Close squadded in the dockyard's hooded lamps,
Each blur a man with some obscure trouble
Or hard regret as bulky as the cargo
The cranking derricks drop into the hold.
Think of them, as the derrick sways and poises
Vacantly as their minds do at this passage,
Good-natured agents of a groping purpose
That sends them now to strange precipitous places
Where all are human and Oh easily hurt
And – the temptation being to forget
Such villages as linger in the mind,
Lidice on the road from Bethlehem –
Ask whether kindness will persist in hearts
Plagued by the snags and rapids of a curse,
And whether the fortunate few will still attain
The sudden flexible grasp of a dangerous problem
And feel their failures broaden into manhood,
Or take the Bren's straightforward road
And grow voluptuous at the sight of blood?
Each of us is invisible to himself,
Our eyes grow neutral in the long Unseen,
We take or do not take a hand of cards,
We shake down nightly in the strange Unknown.
Yet each one has a hankering in the blood,
A dark relation that disturbs his joke
And will not be abandoned with a shrug:
Each has a shrunken inkling of the Good.
And one man, wrapped in blankets, solemnly
Remembers as he bites his trembling nails
The white delightful limbs, the nest of peace.
And one who misses what it's all about,
Sick with injections, sees the 'tween-decks turn
To fields of home, each tree with its rustling shadow
Slipped like a young girl's dress down to its ankles;

114

Where lovers lay in chestnut shadows,
And horses carne there from the burning meadows.
And these things stay, in seasonal rotation
Within the cycles of our false intention.

But others, lacking the power of reflection,
Broke ship, impelled by different emotions.
The police are seeking men of their description
As sedulously as their own promotion.

II

Before he sails a man may go on leave
To any place he likes, where he's unknown
Or where he's mentioned with a warm inflection
And hands are shaken up and down the street.
Some men avoid this act of recognition
And make the world a dartboard for their fling;
Oblivion is the colour of brown ale;
Peace is the backseat in the cinema.
But most men seek the place where they were born.

For me it was a long slow day by train.

Just here you leave this Cardiganshire lane,
Here by these milk churns and this telegraph pole,
Latch up the gate and cut across the fields.
Some things you see in detail, those you need;
The raindrops spurting from the trodden stubble
Squirting your face across the reaping meadow,
The strange machine-shaped scarab beetle
His scalloped legs clung bandy to a stalk,
The Jew's-harp bee with saddlebags of gold,
The wheat as thin as hair on flinty slopes,
The harsh hewn faces of the farming folks,
Opinion humming like a nest of wasps,
The dark-clothed brethren at the chapel gates;

And farther on the mortgaged crumbling farm
Where Shonni Rhys, that rough backsliding man
Has found the sheep again within the corn
And fills the evening with his sour oaths;
The curse of failure's in his shambling gait.

At last the long wet sands, the shelving beach,
The green Atlantic, far as eye can reach.
And what is here but what was always here
These twenty years, elusive as a dream
Flowing between the grinding-stones of fact –
A girl's affections or a new job lost,
A lie that burns the soft stuff in the brain,
Lust unconfessed, a scholarship let go
Or gained too easily, without much point –
Each hurt a search for those old country gods
A man takes with him in his native tongue
Finding a friendly word for all things strange,
The firm authentic truth of roof and rain.
And on the cliff's green brink where nothing stirs,
Unless the wind should stir it, I perceive
A child grow shapely in the loins I love.

III

In all the ways of going who can tell
The real from the unjustified farewell?
Women have sobbed when children left for school
Or husbands took the boat train to pursue
Contracts more tenuous than the marriage vow.
But now each railway station makes and breaks
The certain hold and drifts us all apart.
Some women know exactly what's implied.
Ten Years, they say behind their smiling eyes,
Thinking of children, pensions, looks that fade,
The slow forgetfulness that strips the mind
Of its apparel and wears down the thread;

Or maybe when he laughs and bends to make
Her laugh with him she sees that he must die
Because his eyes declare it plain as day.
And it is here, if anywhere, that words
– Debased like money by the same diseases –
Cast off the habitual clichés of fatigue
– The women hoping it will soon blow over,
The fat men saying it depends on Russia –
And all are poets when they say Goodbye
And what they say will live and fructify.

IV

And so we wait the tide, and when the dark
Laps round the swelling entrance to the sea
The grey evasive ship slips into line.
The bell clangs in the engine room, the night
Shrouds the cold faces watching at the rail.
Till suddenly from headland and from wharves
The searchlights throw their lambent bluish cloaks
Clothing the fairway in a sheen of silk.
The steel bows break, the churning screw burns white.
Each pallid face wears an unconscious smile.
And I – I pray my unborn tiny child
Has five good senses and an earth as kind
As the sweet breast of her who gives him milk
And waves me down this first clandestine mile.

A Troopship in the Tropics

Five thousand souls are here and all are bounded
Too easily perhaps by the ostensible purpose,
Steady as the ploughshare cleaving England,
Of this great ship, obedient to its compass.

The sundeck for the children and the officers
Under the awning, watching the midsea blue
Until the nurses pass with a soft excitement
Rustling the talk of passengers and crew.

Deep in the foetid hold the tiered bunks
Hold restless men who sweat and toss and sob;
The gamblers on the hatches, in the corner
The accordionist and the barber do their job.

The smell of oranges and excrement
Moves among those who write uneasy letters
Or slouch about and curse the stray dejection
That chafes them with its hard nostalgic fetters.

But everywhere in this sweltering Utopia,
In the bareheaded crowd's two minutes' silence,
In corners where the shadows lie like water,
Are tranquil pools of crystal-clear reflexion.

Time is no mystery now; this torrid blueness
Blazed in a fortnight from the English winter.
Distance is subject to our moods and wishes.
Only the void of feeling must be filled.

And as the ship makes peace within herself
The simple donors of goodness with rugged features
Move in the crowd and share their crusts of wisdom;
Life does not name her rough undoctored teachers.

Welsh songs surge softly in the circling darkness;
Thoughts sail back like swans to the English winter;
Strange desires drift into the mind;
Time hardens. But the ruthless Now grows kind.

Chanson Triste

By day the sun ranted
Strode to his zenith
Stared imperturbably
Pitiless conqueror.

And the moon in her gentleness
Softly companions us
Leading us, wayfarers,
Through her white acres.

But how can we sleep
Though the hour is late
Who lost man's fine mastery
Over his fate?

With all that is human
The tall stars decline.
Bitterest agony
Bleeds the divine.

And huge as the shadows
My longing runs wild
Oh world! Oh wanton!
For my woman, my child.

Song

(*On seeing dead bodies floating off the Cape*)

The first month of his absence
I was numb and sick
And where he'd left his promise
Life did not turn or kick.
The seed, the seed of love was sick.

The second month my eyes were sunk
In the darkness of despair,
And my bed was like a grave
And his ghost was lying there.
And my heart was sick with care.

The third month of his going
I thought I heard him say
'Our course deflected slightly
On the thirty-second day –'
The tempest blew his words away.

And he was lost among the waves,
His ship rolled helpless in the sea,
The fourth month of his voyage
He shouted grievously
'Beloved, do not think of me.'

The flying fish like kingfishers
Skim the sea's bewildered crests,
The whales blow steaming fountains,
The seagulls have no nests
Where my lover sways and rests.

We never thought to buy and sell
This life that blooms or withers in the leaf,
And 'll not stir, so he sleeps well,
Though cell by cell the coral reef
Builds an eternity of grief.

But oh! the drag and dullness of my Self;
The turning seasons wither in my head;
All this slowness, all this hardness,
The nearness that is waiting in my bed,
The gradual self-effacement of the dead.

Port of Call: Brazil

We watch the heavy-odoured beast
Of darkness crouch along the water-front
Under the town exorcised by the priest.
The lights entice the paramours to hunt.

Tropical thunder creams the glassy bay,
White sails on bamboo masts disturb the night,
The troopship turns and drags upon her stay,
The portholes cast a soft, subjective light.

And we who crowd in hundreds to the side
Feel the lights prick us with a grey distaste
As though we had some guilty thing to hide –
We, who thought the negroes were debased

This morning when they scrambled on the quay
For what we threw, and from their dugout boats
Haggled cigars and melons raucously
Lifting their bleating faces like old goats.

But now the white-faced tourist must translate
His old unsated longing to adventure
Beyond the European's measured hate
Into the dangerous oceans of past and future

Where trembling intimations will reveal
The illusion of this blue mulatto sleep
And in that chaos like a migrant eel
Will breed a new direction through the deep.

Part Three: India

To Rilke

Rilke, if you had known that I was trying
To speak to you perhaps you would have said
'Humanity has her darlings to whom she's entrusted
A farthing maybe, or a jewel, at least a perception
Of what can develop and what must be always endured
And what the live may answer to the dead.
Such ones are known by their faces,
At least their absence is noted;
And they never lack an occasion,
They, the devoted.'

But I have to seek the occasion.
Labour, fatigue supervene;
The glitter of sea and land, the self-assertion
These fierce competing times insist upon.

Yet sometimes, seeking, hours glided inwards,
Laying their soft antennae on my heart,
And I forgot the thousand leagues I'd journeyed
As if Creation were about to start.

I watched the pure horizon for the earth
To rise in grey bare peaks that might enfold
The empty crumbling soil between the hands
Or coloured things a child's small fist might hold
Delightedly; I knew that unknown lands
Were near and real, like an act of birth.

Then I fell ill and restless.
Sweating and febrile all one burning week,
I hungered for the silence you acquired
And *envied* you, as though it were a gift
Presented on a birthday to the lucky.
For that which IS I thought you need not seek.

The sea is gone now and the crowded tramp
Sails other seas with other passengers.
I sit within the tent, within the darkness
Of India, and the wind disturbs my lamp.

The jackals howl and whimper in the nullah,
The goatherd sleeps upon a straw-piled bed,
And I know that in this it does not matter
Where one may be or what fate lies ahead.

And Vishnu, carved by some rude pious hand,
Lies by a heap of stones, demanding nothing
But the simplicity that she and I
Discovered in a way you'd understand
Once and for ever, Rilke, but in Oh a distant land.

By the Gateway of India: Bombay

The storm's cold javelins constrain
The swirling roads, the anchored fleet
Curled in Elephanta's lee
Where pilgrims walked on naked feet:
 – And in the darkness did they see
The darker terrors of the brain?
And did the hollow oracle resound
In caves of unexpected pain?
And were they drenched as we who loiter
Beneath the Imperial Gate
By the biting arrows of the rain?
And did they also hate?

We who let the evening come
Have our peculiar pride, never to flinch;
Our dignity has schooled us to submit:
Life has withdrawn its word, the day has gone,
But we contest the darkness inch by inch.
And though the starving outcasts tell
The imminent peril of the state
We are incredulous of fate.

A red-winged gull beats down the bay,
Finds the mole, the square of green,
And shakes the tempest off its breast.
But we who with the beggars lean
Against the indifferent arch of kings
Infected with the crowd's unrest
And remembering younger springs,
Tie the aching knots of lust
In the harlot's clinging breath,

Knowing life and knowing death.

The Way Back

Six days and two thousand miles
I have watched the shafted rain
Feminise the burning land,
Cloaking with a green distress
The cerulean and the ochre
Of the season's ruthlessness.

Six days and two thousand miles
I have gone alone
With a green mind and you
Burning in the stubborn bone.

Soldiers quickened by your breath
Feel the sudden spur and rush
Of the life they put away
Lest the war should break and crush
Beauties more profound than death.

I swam within your naked lake
And breasted with exquisite ease
The foaming arabesques of joy
And in the sarabande of trees
Of guava and papaya
And crimson blown poinsettia,
The millrace of my blood
Beat against my smile,
And were you answering my smile
Or the millrace of my blood?

But now the iron beasts deploy
And all my effort is my fate
With gladiators and levies
All laconic disciplined men
I pass beyond your golden gate.

And in the hardness of this world
And in the brilliance of this pain
I exult with such a passion
To be squandered, to be hurled,
To be joined to you again.

Karanje Village

The sweeper said Karanje had a temple
A roof of gold in the gaon:
But I saw only the long-nosed swine and the vultures
Groping the refuse for carrion,
And the burial cairns on the hill with its spout of dust
Where the mules stamp and graze,
The naked children begging, the elders in poverty,
The sun's dry beat and glaze,

The crumbling hovels like a discredited fortress,
The old hags mumbling by the well,
The young girls in purple always avoiding us,
The monkeys loping obscenely round our smell –

– The trees were obscene with the monkeys' grey
        down-hanging
Their long slow leaping and stare,
The girl in a red sari despairingly swinging her rattle,
The sacred monkeys mocking all her care.

And alone by a heap of stones in the lonely salt plain
A little Vishnu of stone,
Silently and eternally simply Being,
Bidding me come alone,

And never entirely turning me away,
But warning me still of the flesh
That catches and limes the singing birds of the soul
And holds their wings in mesh.

But the people are hard and hungry and have no love
Diverse and alien, uncertain in their hate,
Hard stones flung out of Creation's silent matrix,
And the Gods must wait.
And Love must wait, as the unknown yellow poppy
Whose lovely fragile petals are unfurled
Among the lizards in this wasted land.

And when my sweetheart calls me shall I tell her
That I am seeking less and less of world?
And will she understand?

The Mahratta Ghats

The valleys crack and burn, the exhausted plains
Sink their black teeth into the horny veins
Straggling the hills' red thighs, the bleating goats –
– Dry bents and bitter thistles in their throats –
Thread the loose rocks by immemorial tracks.
Dark peasants drag the sun upon their backs.

High on the ghat the new turned soil is red,
The sun has ground it to the finest red,
It lies like gold within each horny hand.
Siva has spilt his seed upon this land.

Will she who burns and withers on the plain
Leave, ere too late, her scraggy herds of pain,
The cow-dung fire and the trembling beasts,
The little wicked gods, the grinning priests,
And climb, before a thousand years have fled,
High as the eagle to her mountain bed
Whose soil is fine as flour and blood-red?

But no! She cannot move. Each arid patch
Owns the lean folk who plough and scythe and thatch
Its grudging yield and scratch its stubborn stones.
The small gods suck the marrow from their bones.

Who is it climbs the summit of the road?
Only the beggar bumming his dark load.
Who was it cried to see the falling star?
Only the landless soldier lost in war.

And did a thousand years go by in vain?
And does another thousand start again?

'Holi'

(The Hindu festival of Spring)

The village is growing fertile,
The bankrupt peasant feels the wheat
Spring green within his stony loins,
All night the sweating drumsticks beat.

The girls with priestly faces
Stir in the circle of flame.
Red ochre melts on their foreheads,
Their eyes are dark with shame.

The drum beats a crescendo,
The young men are fain,
The moon is swollen in the forest
The young girls twitch with pain.

Blood drips from the drumskins,
The youths and girls obey
The wild God's uttermost intent,
And sob, and turn away,

And turn to the Indian forest
And there they are as one –
One with the dust and darkness
When the God's last will is done.

The Journey

We were the fore-runners of an army,
Going among strangers without sadness,
Danger being as natural as strangeness.

We had no other urge but to compel
Tomorrow in the image of today,
Which was motion and mileage and tinkering
When cylinders misfired and the gasket leaked.
Distance exhausted us each night;
I curled up in the darkness like a dog
And being a romantic stubbed my eyes
Upon the wheeling spoke shave of the stars.
Daylight had girls tawny as gazelles,
Beating their saris clean in pools and singing.
When we stopped they covered up their breasts;
Sometimes their gestures followed us for miles.

Then caravanserais of gipsies
With donkeys grey as mice and mincing camels
Laden with new-born lambs and trinkets,
Tentage and utensils and wicker baskets,
Following the ancient routes of the vast migrations
When history was the flight of a million birds
And poverty had splendid divagations.

Sometimes there were rivers that refused us,
Sweeping away the rafts, the oxen;
Some brown spates we breasted.
The jungle let us through with compass and machets.
And there were men like fauns, with drenched eyes,
Avoiding us, bearing arrows.

There was also the memory of Death
And the recurrent irritation of our selves.
But the wind so wound its ways about us,
Beyond this living and this loving,
This calculation and provision, this fearing,

That neither of us heard the quiet voice calling us,
Remorse like rain softening and rotting the ground,
We felt no sorrow in the singing bird,
Forgot the sadness we had left behind.
For how could we guess, oh Life, oh suffering and
patient Life,
With distance spun for ever in the mind,
We among the camels, the donkeys and the waterfalls,
How could we ever guess,
Not knowing how you pined?

Ways

I

It had been easier, not loving.

I knew I had grown harder than the trees
In which I held you all the afternoon,
The tall blue slender saplings leaning
Each on each, their strength outgrowing.
And suddenly we two were swaying
Each upon the other leaning.

It had been easier, not loving.

II

It was much easier, all alone.

The tall slim saplings were exhausted so
With tallness and with slenderness they bowed
At the touch of wind or bird.
And the lightness of your hands
Bowed me also with their guerdon,
Love being gravel in the wound
When the silent lovers know
Swaying in the misty rain
The old oppression of the burden
Growing in them as they go,
Though trees are felled and grow again,
Far and farther each from each.
Longing hardens like a stone.

Lovers go but hardly, all alone.

Village Funeral: Maharashtra

The wasted sleepy corpse
Benignly, unassumingly reposes
Among the flowers flung on him all day.
The cowdung fire decomposes.

The drum denies identity,
The patient elements ignite,
Life stirs and shifts and gradually breaks
Within the burning night.

This dead man is no more.
Silence fills the throbbing drum,
Dries the sweat on every face,
Mutely bids the dayspring come.

Nandi, bull of holiness,
Ganpati, elephantine force,
Siva, destroyer and sparer,
Consider this poor corpse.

Not being and then being,
– Cowdung fire, bed of earth, –
How shall the peasant fare between
One birth and another birth?

Water Music

Deep in the heart of the lake
Where the last light is clinging
A strange foreboding voice
Is patiently singing.

Do not fear to venture
Where the last light trembles
Because you were in love.
Love never dissembles.

Fear no more the boast, the bully,
The lies, the vain labour.
Make no show for death
As for a rich neighbour.

What stays of the great religions?
An old priest, an old birth.
What stays of the great battles?
Dust on the earth.

Cold is the lake water
And dark as history.
Hurry not and fear not
This oldest mystery.

This strange voice singing,
This slow deep drag of the lake,
This yearning, yearning, this ending
Of the heart and its ache.

Shadows

The moon turns round the earth
And the earth turns round the sun;
In gold and white infinities
Their timeless task is done.

Under the shadow of the earth
The moon in crescent stays,
Dark as an untended wound
Despite the splendid phrase.

Love reeled in that dark, and beauty
Stained the rocks with fragile flowers.
But love and beauty will survive
These grey malignant hours.

Strangeness does not make me strange.
Of strangers born I know that good
Lay with evil in the hedge.
The rest is in the mood.

He chooses best who does not choose
Time and all its lies;
Who makes the end and the beginning One
Within himself, grows wise.

The cold winds of indifference
Disturb the scarves of night,
As earth and moon go voyaging
Through dark, through light.

Home Thoughts from Abroad

As if the ant should fail with desire
And cast her chiffon wings and groan,
The trumpet's warm and selfish lusts
Occlude this breathless Indian night.
The trumpeter stands alone.

Oh West, your blue nostalgic moods
Confuse the troubled continents.
The shaven-headed prisoners moan
And girls with serpents at their breasts
And boys with dead hands on their knees
Lie stricken in your scattered tents.

And we who feel the darkness twitch
With death among the orange trees
Seek, and not in vain, your hills
Whose bridle paths all end in dark
And find love in the gap of centuries
Although the swart brown heather bears no mark
Of boy and girl and all they planned.

We surely were not hard to please
And yet you cast us out. And in this land
We bear the dark inherited disease
Bred in the itching warmness of your hand.

In Hospital: Poona (I)

Last night I did not fight for sleep
But lay awake from midnight while the world
Turned its slow features to the moving deep
Of darkness, till I knew that you were furled,

Beloved, in the same dark watch as I.
And sixty degrees of longitude beside
Vanished as though a swan in ecstasy
Had spanned the distance from your sleeping side.

And like to swan or moon the whole of Wales
Glided within the parish of my care:
I saw the green tide leap on Cardigan,
Your red yacht riding like a legend there,
And the great mountains, Dafydd and Llewelyn,
Plynlimmon, Cader Idris and Eryri
Threshing the darkness back from head and fin,
And also the small nameless mining valley

Whose slopes are scratched with streets and
        sprawling graves
Dark in the lap of firwoods and great boulders
Where you lay waiting, listening to the waves–
My hot hands touched your white despondent shoulders

– And then ten thousand miles of daylight grew
Between us, and I heard the wild daws crake
In India's starving throat; whereat I knew
That Time upon the heart can break
But love survives the venom of the snake.

In Hospital: Poona (2)

The sun has sucked and beat the encircling hills
Into gaunt skeletons; the sick men watch
Soft shadows warm those bones of rock,
And the barefooted peasants winding back,
Sad withered loins in hanging dirty folds,
Mute sweepings from the disappointed streets,
Old shrunken tribes the starving dusk enfolds.
The wind sweeps up the rifle range and blows
The Parsis' long white robes, there where they go
Under the wheeling kites, bearing a corpse
To the high tower that the vultures know.

And from the polished ward where men lie ill
Thought rubs clean through the frayed cloth of the will,

Piercing the slow estrangement of disease,
And breaks into a state of blinding light
Where Now is a salt pillar, still and white,
And there are no familiar words or features
Nor blood nor tears no joy nor living creatures,
A void where Pain demands no cheap release
But white and rigid freezes into peace,
And mind lies coiled within green icebound streams
And sheds the stippled scales of ancient dreams.

And by that Arctic silence overawed
The mind crawls wounded from the lidless God,
And breeds again the hope that has no food
But lives amongst the evil and the good,
Biding its time amongst the lives that fail
While darkness crowds its dark piratic sail.
Yet in the garden of the hospital
The moonlight spills and sings in a stone pool,
Allowing those who loiter to recall
That which the whiplash sun drove out of bounds –
The heart's calm voice that stills the baying hounds.

Indian Day

I

Dawn's cold imperative compels
Bazaars and gutters to disturb
Famine's casual ugly tableaux.
Lazarus is lifted from the kerb.

The supple sweeper girl goes by
Brushing the dung of camels from the street
The daylight's silver bangles
Glitter on her naked feet.

II

Yellow ramtilla stiffens in the noon,
Jackals skulk among the screes,
In skinny fields the oxen shiver,
The gods have prophesied disease.

Hedges of spike and rubber, hedges of cactus,
Lawns of bougainvillia, jasmine, zinnia,
Terraces of privelege and loathing,
The masterly shadows of a nightmare

Harden and grow lengthy in the drought.
The moneyed antipathetic faces
Converse in courts of pride and fountains
With ermined sleek injustices.
Gods and dacoits haunt the mountains.

III

The sun the thunder and the hunger grow
Extending stupidly the helds of pain
Ploughing the peasant under with his crop
Denying the great mercy of the rain

Denying what each flowering pear and lime
And every child and each embrace imply –
The love that is imprisoned in each heart
By the famines and fortunes of the century.

IV

Night bibles India in her wilderness
The Frontier Mail screams blazing with such terror
The russet tribesman lays aside his flute
Rigid with Time's hypnotic surging error.

The kindness of the heart lies mute
Caught in the impotence of dreams
Yet all night long the boulders sing
The timeless songs of mountain streams.

The Peasants

The dwarf barefooted, chanting
Behind the oxen by the lake,
Stepping lightly and lazily among the thorntrees
Dusky and dazed with sunLight, half awake;

The women breaking stones upon the highway,
Walking erect with burdens on their heads,
One body growing in another body,
Creation touching verminous straw beds.

Across scorched hills and trampled crops
The soldiers straggle by.
History staggers in their wake.
The peasants watch them die.

Observation Post: Forward Area

The thorns are bleached and brittle,
The empty folds decay,
Rooftrees creak in the silence
Of inarticulate dismay.

Drought denudes the planting;
In the dry red heat
Dawn spills its ghostly water,
Black heads on the wheat.

Some evil presence quenches
The vagrant drunken theme
Of the swart and skinny goatherd
And the black goats of his dream.

A darker beast than poverty
Transfixed the crouching peasants there,
And tore the votive tablets down
And filled the children with such fear.

The cowdung fires guttered out,
The wizened women cried,
The bridegroom lay trembling,
And rigid the bride.

Love could be had for nothing.
And where is love now?
Gone with the shambling oxen,
Gone with the broken plough,
Death lives here now.

Burma Casualty

(To Capt. G.T. Morris, Indian Army)

I

Three endless weeks of sniping all the way,
Lying up when their signals rang too close,
– 'Ooeee, Ooee,' like owls, the lynx-eyed Jap, –
Sleeplessly watching, knifing, falling back.
And now the Sittang river was there at last
And the shambles of trucks and corpses round the bridge
And the bridge was blown. And he laughed.

And then a cough of bullets, a dusty cough
Filleted all his thigh from knee to groin.
The kick of it sucked his face into the wound.
He crumpled, thinking 'Death'. But no, not yet.
The femoral artery wasn't touched.
Great velour cloaks of darkness floated up.
But he refused, refused the encircling dark,
A lump of bitter gristle that refused.
The day grew bloodshot as they picked him up.

II

Lying in hospital he often thought
Of that darkness, whence it came
And how it played the enchantress in a grain
Of morphia or a nodding of the head
Late in the night and offered to release
The Beast that breathed with pain and ran with pus
Among the jumping fibres of the flesh.
And then he saw the Padre by his cot
With the Last Unction: and he started up.

III

'Your leg must go. Okay?' the surgeon said
'Take it' he said. 'I hate the bloody thing.'
Yet he was terrified – not of the knives
Nor loosing that green leg (he'd often wished
He'd had a gun to shoot the damned thing off)
But of the darkness that he knew would come
And bid him enter its deep gates alone.

The nurse would help him and the orderlies.
But did they know? And could a rubber tube
Suck all that darkness out of lungs and heart?
'Open and close your fist – slowly,' the doctor said.
He did so, lying still upon his back.
The whitewashed walls, the windows bright with sky
Gathered a brilliant light above his head.
Here was the light, the promise hard and pure,
His wife's sweet body and her wilful eyes.
Her timeless love stooped down to raise him up.
He felt the white walls part – the needle pricked,
'Ten seconds and you'll fade,' the doctor said.
He lay and looked into the snowwhite skies
For all ten seconds means at such a time.
Then through the warped interstices of life
The darkness swept like water through a boat
In gouts and waves of softness, claiming him...

He went alone: knew nothing: and returned
Retching and blind with pain, and yet Alive.

IV

Mending, with books and papers and a fan
Sunlight on parquet floors and bowls of flame
He heard quite casually that his friends were dead,

His regiment too butchered to reform.
And he lay in the lightness of the ward
Thinking of all the lads the dark enfolds
So secretly.
          And yet a man may walk
Into and through it, and return alive.
Why had his friends all stayed there, then?
He knew.
The dark is a beautiful singing sexless angel
Her hands so soft you scarcely feel her touch
Gentle, eternally gentle, round your heart.
She flatters and unsexes every man.

And Life is only a crude, pigheaded churl
Frowsy and starving, daring to suffer alone.

The Unknown Soldier

Everything has lasted till today.
He stares upon it like a velvet king.
Velasquez might have made this flaccid mask,
The silence round the languid mouth,
The weak and glassy eyes, the crumpled brow.
All things are out-distanced now.

All days are heaped in wrath upon today.
The senses sleep except one crazy spark
That leaps the lesion slashed between his eyes
And cries – not for a fertile century,
Nor for the secular ransom of the soul –
But for a sip of water from my flask.
What is the soul to him?
He has outlasted everything.

Joy's deceitfull liturgy has ceased.
Tomorrow and tomorrow have no place
Among the seas of rain, the seas of peace
That are the elements of this poor face.
The mean humiliating self no more
Has access to him, nor the friends
Whose sensual persuasions first began
The brittle scattering that this day ends.
On pander, lord and jester slams the door.
And impotent in his kingdom the grey king
No longer clings to that which dies.

He has abandoned everything.
Velasquez, close those doglike dolorous eyes.

Peasant Song

The seed is costly
Sow it carefully
I have only this small plough
To turn the mighty earth.

And will you kiss me now
And with mysterious birth
Bless this hut of rod and reed
And I will turn the mighty earth
And you will hold the seed?

And if sun and rain are kind
The young green crops will grow
More abundant than my mind
Swaying where the cattle graze

But if I should go
And you be left behind
Among the tall red ant hills and the maize
Would you hear my plough still singing
And, bearing endless days,
Somehow give praise?

Wood Song

The pine trees cast their needles softly
Darling for your gipsy bed
And the tall blue saplings swaying
Whisper more than can be said.

Piteously the world is happening
Beyond this cool stockade of trees
Enduring passions penetrate
These quiet rides with agonies
That love can never consummate.

And we must go because we love
Beyond ourselves, beyond these trees
That sway above your golden head
Till wind and war and sky and dove
Become again the murmur of your breath
And your body the white shew-bread.

The Island

I watched your houseboat, young patrician,
Cast off the island and attempt the bay,
I knew it was no routine trip to purchase
The island's meat and bread for one more day.

Garlanded, you paid away like rope
The island's mastery, only achieved
The moment you forsook it; I discerned
A woman standing dull as the bereaved.

And now the mainland takes you with its hunger
And as your boat jerks crunching on the shore
Do you step off fastidious as a virgin,
Or with the mute complaisance of a whore?

And were you taught what words are expeditious
What sins are venial, what are held in shame?
And have you sipped the blue bouquet of power
And were you humble when they promised fame?

How will you meet the first appraising glances
Of the anonymous strangers in the street?
Do you grow fierce within the toils of pity?
And know the millions you will never meet?

And do you in this piteous human flux
Possess the high imponderable art
To turn us by a hair's-breadth in our trouble
To greater agony or joy of heart?

I only watched you landing and I know not.
But this I know, that were I in your stead,
I would not change the island that holds nothing,
For these rich mines of silver and of lead
And these pale girls whose hearts are with the dead.

Motifs

The tide is slack in equipoise,
Lapping the inmost reaches of the creek.
Beyond the bar's white rip the fishermen
Trim their torn sails on blocks that swell and creak
And gather in the strange cold life they seek.

Dry as a lizard, lazy on the foreshore,
I hear the harsh cicadas' monody,
And knowing there is little but this sunlight
These desultory palms, this tepid sea,
I bid Love ask no further proof of me.

In high conjunction sun and moon
Drive the spring tides across the muddy land.
The close and sentient mind is helpless here,
And I who do not fully understand,
But half forgetting, half expecting lie
And let the world fall softly from my hand,
Conceal my heart's great love and love's great fear,
And would forget you, if I could, my dear.

Bivouac

There was no trace of Heaven
That night as we lay
Punch-drunk and blistered with sunlight
On the ploughed-up clay.

I remembered the cactus where our wheels
Had bruised it, bleeding white;
And a fat rat crouching beadyeyed
Caught by my light;

And the dry disturbing whispers
Of the agitated wood,
With its leathery vendetta,
Mantillas dark with blood.

And the darkness drenched with Evil
Haunting as a country song,
Ignoring the protesting cry
Of Right and of Wrong.

Yet the peasant was drawing water
With the first excited bird
And the dawn with childish eyes
Observed us as we stirred

And the milk-white oxen waited
Docile at the yoke
As we clipped on our equipment
And scarcely spoke

Being bewildered by the night
And only aware
Of the withering obsession
That lovers grow to fear
When the last note is written
And at last and alone
One of them wakes in terror
And the other is gone.

The Jungle

I

In mole-blue indolence the sun
Plays idly on the stagnant pool
In whose grey bed black swollen leaf
Holds Autumn rotting like an unfrocked priest.
The crocodile slides from the ochre sand
And drives the great translucent fish
Under the boughs across the running gravel.
Windfalls of brittle mast crunch as we come
To quench more than our thirst – our selves –
Beneath this bamboo bridge, this mantled pool
Where sleep exudes a sinister content
As though all strength of mind and limb must pass
And all fidelities and doubts dissolve,
The weighted world a bubble in each head,
The warm pacts of the flesh betrayed
By the nonchalance of a laugh,
The green indifference of this sleep.

II

Wandering and fortuitous the paths
We followed to this rendezvous today
Out of the mines and offices and dives,
The sidestreets of anxiety and want,
Huge cities known and distant as the stars,
Wheeling beyond our destiny and hope.
We did not notice how the accent changed
As shadows ride from precipice to plain
Closing the parks and cordoning the roads,
Clouding the humming cultures of the West –
The weekly bribe we paid the man in black,
The day shift sinking from the sun,
The blinding arc of rivets blown through steel,
The patient queues, headlines and slogans flung

Across a frightened continent, the town
Sullen and out of work, the little home
Semi-detached, suburban, transient
As fever or the anger of the old,
The best ones on some specious pretext gone.

But we who dream beside this jungle pool
Prefer the instinctive rightness of the poised
Pied kingfisher deep darting for a fish
To all the banal rectitude of states,
The dew-bright diamonds on a viper's back
To the slow poison of a meaning lost
And the vituperations of the just.

III

The banyan's branching clerestories close
The noon's, harsh splendour to a head of light.
The black spot in the focus grows and grows:
The vagueness of the child, the lover's deep
And inarticulate bewilderment,
The willingness to please that made a wound,
The kneeling darkness and the hungry prayer;
Cargoes of anguish in the holds of joy,
The smooth deceitful stranger in the heart,
The tangled wrack of motives drifting down
An oceanic tide of Wrong.
And though the state has enemies we know
The greater enmity within ourselves.

Some things we cleaned like knives in earth,
Kept from the dew and rust of Time
Instinctive truths and elemental love,
Knowing the force that brings the teal and quail
From Turkestan across the Himalayan snows
To Kashmir and the South alone can guide
That winging wildness home again.

Oh you who want us for ourselves,
Whose love can start the snow-rush in the woods
And melt the glacier in the dark coulisse,
Forgive this strange inconstancy of soul,
The face distorted in a jungle pool
That drowns its image in a mort of leaves.

IV

Grey monkeys gibber, ignorant and wise.
We are the ghosts, and they the denizens;
We are like them anonymous, unknown,
Avoiding what is human, near,
Skirting the villages, the paddy fields
Where boys sit timelessly to scare the crows
On bamboo platforms raised above their lives.

A trackless wilderness divides
Joy from its cause, the motive from the act:
The killing arm uncurls, strokes the soft moss;
The distant world is an obituary,
We do not hear the tappings of its dread.
The act sustains; there is no consequence.
Only aloneness, swinging slowly
Down the cold orbit of an older world
Than any they predicted in the schools,
Stirs the cold forest with a starry wind,
And sudden as the flashing of a sword
The dream exalts the bowed and golden head
And time is swept with a great turbulence,
The old temptation to remould the world.

The bamboos creak like an uneasy house;
The night is shrill with crickets, cold with space.
And if the mute pads on the sand should lift
Annihilating paws and strike us down
Then would some unimportant death resound

With the imprisoned music of the soul?
And we become the world we could not change?
Or does the will's long struggle end
With the last kindness of a foe or friend?

The Assault Convoy

Three days of waiting in the islands
Of a remote inhospitable bay
Have soured the small dry stretch of time
Which we allow to drift away
Disconsolate that death should so delay

His wild and breathless act upon the fore-shore
The seas still separate and hide.
Our hobnails stamp in crazy repetition,
Bodies' sweat to bodies' sweat confide
The intimacy we denied.

The nihilist persistence of the sun,
The engines throbbing heatedly all night,
The white refineries of salt and dust
Forbid the mind to think, the pen to write;
We trample down the fences of delight.

Perhaps the ultimate configuration
Of island and peninsula and reef
Will have the same shapes, tortuous and crannied
And the same meaning as our dark belief,
The solid contours of our native grief.
The real always fades into the meaning,
From cone to thread some grave perception drives
The twisted failures into vast fulfilments.
After the holocaust of shells and knives,
The victory, the treaty, the betrayal,
The supersession of a million lives,
The hawk sees something stir among the trenches,
The field mouse hears the sigh of what survives.

The Raid

The estuary silted up
The dredger rusting by the pier
The beaches red and indolent
The coolies running now with fear.

This complex expedition
Calculated, intricate,
Spills blood and pain and agony
Carefully discounting Fate.

And the needed devotion
Of terrified boys
Spreadeagles the horror
That annuls and destroys

The calm intimations
Of lamplight on books,
The warm naked shoulder,
The harvest in stooks.

And racked with the passion
That Life should have done,
The bleeding entrails tremble
In the merciless sun

That beats on the silted up the river,
The rusty dredger, the pier,
The indolent red beaches,
The confusion, the fear.

A Fragment

Where aloneness fiercely
Trumpets the unsounded night
And the silence surges higher
Than hands or seas or mountains' height

I the deep shaft sinking
Through the quivering Unknown
Feel your anguish beat its answer
As you grow round me, flesh and bone.

The wild beast in the cave
Is all our pride; and will not be
Again until the world's blind travail
Breaks in crimson flower from the tree

I am, in Thee.

Midnight in India

Here is no mined and cratered deep
As in the fenced-off landscapes of the West
Within this Eastern wilderness
The human war is lost.

The three dark quarters bow their heads
To where the fourth in radiance glows;
The withered villages look up and smile;
The moon's annunciation grows.

Oh I have set the earth aflame
And brought the high dominions down,
And soiled each simple act with shame
And had no feelings of my own.

I sank in drumming tides of grief
And in the sea-king's sandy bed
Submerged in gulfs of disbelief
Lay with the redtoothed daughters of the dead.

Until you woke me with a sigh
And eased the dark compression in my head
And sang and did not cease when I
Broke your heart like holy bread.

We cast away the bitter death
That holds the fine circumference of life
And gathered in a single breath
All that begins and ends in man and wife

And though the painful errors grow
And youth sprawls dead beside the Gate
And lovely bodies stiffen in the snow
And old devotions breed a newer hate,

Yet time stands still upon the east
The moonlight lies in pools and human pain
Soothes the dry lips on which it lies
And I behold your calm white face again.

Mysterious tremors stir the beast,
In unknown worlds he dies;
I lie within your hands, within your peace,
And watch this last effulgent world arise.

Uncollected Poems

The Slug

The slug had climbed, when first I shut the door,
An inch above the skirting, scarcely more.
Now, when I pause, I see the silver line
Its belly's sweat has made to mark its climb
Up to the ceiling, all its night-long strife
Betokened in one sticky slot of life.

And I am dull and jaded from this night I've spent alone
Fretting over sins for which no fretting can atone.

But all my anguish leaves no trace to show
My brother slug the bitter way I go
To ceilings which I sense but cannot see –

What earthly use can pen and paper be?

Song

O have you seen the thorn that grows
An angry red,
On briars when the frail wood rose
Is dead?

O have you seen the sly rat go,
Soft, sneaking-pawed,
Fearing the ever-threatening blow,
Outlawed?

And can you tell me why it should be so?
And must ever be so?
Such beauty intermingled
With such woe?

The Quest

I cannot see objectively
Those things that are a part of me –
Mudcaked wains, ramshackle sheds,
Grey rain dripping from the leads,
Black ash buds, and sticky leaves,
The slender web the spider weaves,
The reedy lake that gathers up
The day's last radiance in its cup –

But the bright things imaged there
Have knowledge that I cannot share.

Monologue

Mother, will you come
And kiss away my fear,
Every night like this night?
Yes, I will come, my dear.

Tomorrow – do not cry –
Flowers I will bring,
And our secret lullaby
In your ears I'll sing.

Now sleep. Hard shines the moon,
And I must go.
Your narrow bed will soon
Be white with snow.

Belief

In medieval churches those stained glass windows I love best
Whose fragments, shattered once, have been replaced without
    design,
And no longer show the benefactors walking with the Blest;
But crimson, blue, and orange mingled in pellucid splendour
    shine
Bright bits of broken beauty pulsing in veins of lead
For generations after the cursed iconoclasts are dead.

I think humanity will also in that same manner keep
Its innate beauty though the big guns mangle
The delicate limbs of lovers. Somehow, deep
Below the gore and sweat, the bloody tangle
Of passions, entrails, nerves that the politicians leave,
Beauty survives immaculate, though all her lovers grieve.

Olwen and Taliesin

(for two voices)

Olwen:

She said 'Where is the horseman,
Kilhwch with the burning hand,
To take my corpse and cover it
Upon the stony land?'

Taliesin:

His bones are biding their time in Camelot's sunless combe.
For time is on the side of Wales: in Dyfed and in Lleyn
The honeysuckle nods in silence all along the singing lane.

Olwen:

She said 'Where are the shepherd hordes
Of Cader and Plinlymmon, they
Who vainly hacked their bitter swords
On ramparts built in the Byzantine way?'

Taliesin:

Their bones are biding their time in Harlech's stony tomb.
For time is on the side of Wales: in Dyfed and in Lleyn
The honeysuckle nods in silence all along the singing lane.

Olwen:

She said 'Are you a limping prince?
Or do the poor course greyhounds these stale days?
And is a bee's sting in your honeyed tongue?
Then stab me with your praise.'

Taliesin:

They are hacking the English coal in Morgannwg's rifled womb.
But time is on the side of Wales: in Dyfed and in Lleyn
The honeysuckle nods in silence all along the singing lane.

Olwen:

She said 'The poet's mind is dark with lies;
Worms rob the honeycomb in Kilhwch's head;
And summer flowers mock my haggard eyes.
I shall die chaste,' she said.

Taliesin:

The water drips the stone away in Ystradfellte's gloom;
Stone eyelids crack and crumble with staring out their doom.

For time is on the side of Wales: in Dyfed and in Lleyn
The honeysuckle nods in silence all along the singing lane.

The Tiger of Camden Town

Eternal tiger, fretting in the dark,
Moaning, clawing the cage's bars,
Padding about the straw on restless paws,
With lonely glazing eyes.
The keeper is sleeping and the zoo unlit,
The author of the Bestiary is dead,
All is forgotten, lapsed; yet in your dark
Burn jungle lusts and unforgotten scents
That clung to mango boles and bamboo leaves
Over the delicate spoor of the fleeting prey.
Your lust consumes the object of its thirst
In the dark mind alone, your sabre teeth
Crunch on each other in the sickly dark;
And for your lust you get a dole of meat,
Weighed and delivered at the proper hour.

Night-time is torture in the lonely cage,
Watching the wheeling stars, the neutral sky
Severed by steel; and when the sun burns fierce
Loud leering trippers putrefy the day.
Oh God! The soul's a tiger – such a beast
Would ravage all things if he were released.

Lament

Oh Absalom, beloved, what can I say?
– I who stand here so lonely, with my heart like a strange
      child against my breast?
For Love has been sung enough, its tenderness, its pity,
Its passion and its chastity, its sun and moon;
And how can I talk of my heart's dead weight of anguish,
This brutal disgusting oppression that sets me trembling,
Tugging my sinews, choking and drying my mouth?
I am possessed, Absalom, possessed and alone,
And I fight to be free of that which I do not know.

The hermit and the nomad are exalted by loneliness:
And should the runner stay his race to dally by the road?
The lonely trafficker seeks no bounds to the ocean
And runs to no harbour, but goes steadily the way of the
      black swan.

Loneliness is the edge of the wind, the poise of the flower,
And the imagination is lonely at the great thought of death.
But I love the warm rock where we played as children
And the pool where the women wash linen and gossip,
And this tree in whose bark so many have carved their names.
Therefore I am like a lazar outside a house of music
And my knuckles bleed with beating on your shuttered
      window, oh my love.
Yet you will not open, for your house is empty.
Oh Absalom, beloved, how shall I live?

Once in the old days we cherished our anguish,
Defying our foes and daring to travel
Through the heart's ambush.
But now that the world is shattered and the villages ruined
And all the beauty of the people is slandered and spilt,
When blood and ashes are the relic of power
And the pines have no music though the night be cold;
When events are bitter and truth is anguish,
      And you are dead, oh Absalom, my love,

Will the frayed fleece of words keep the cold from my bones?
And will you never some back by moonlight, Absalom,
To blow on these ashes and kindle my flame?

The Swimmer

Early, before the soldiers are awake
Or clogs go clattering from Morfa farm,
Before the red cock lifts his saurian head
Above the nettles on the whitewashed wall
And shakes the hens down from the apple trees,
I take the path, grown tricky in the rain,
Disused these last few years, all overgrown,
And scramble down the green walls of the Cwm
Across the cliff-top fields whose stony yield
Of niggard oats is hunched in dripping sheaves,
Till from a lip of shale the streaming bay
Grinds my cold ears like seashells in the traeth.

I strip, and poise, and plunge into the waves.
In the full ground-swell and the counter swell
Among the rocky channels off the Crib
Naked I flow, yet clear defined, my limbs
Laughing within the laughter of the sea.
My wet black head turns slowly in the swirl,
Leisurely as a seal, considering
The sea's four quarters and the cormorants.

So satisfied I pick my soft-foot way
Up the crustacean rocks towards my clothes.
And in the rough green contact of the grass
Find my continuum and think of friends
Who died in deserts where I also go,
Shivering and sure of what runs on and on.

On the Welsh Mountains

To note precisely all I know
From this high mountain ledge:
The drab streets hacked across the cwm,
Red ruck of rails, abandoned shaft,
Grey Hebron in a rigid cramp,
White cheapjack picture-house, the Church
An old sow stretched beside the stream,
My uncle's house in Milton Street,
Back gardens row on row,
Old thorntrees stunted by the wind,
The new building of the Labour Exchange:
All moving me more, oh much more,
Than the pigeons cleaving and furling
And all traditional beauty....

Deliberately to understate:
To pare down to the quick
Reality; to be
In love articulate.

The misty rain slants on my skin.
I am forced to imagine
A sea-surge in this bony valley,
The wind-tide and the mermaid
May-blossom nonchalantly swaying
Nibbling the sweet tips of catkin coral
As I approach her swaying,
Her curled attraction –
Till my fingers
Lambent in her maiden hair,
Play simple strange
Chromatic scales.
I wake
The ache of lovers drifted deep
In the nakedness of flowers where
The blue sea-holly holds itself
Against its white assailant from the sea.

And as I play, on my dry scales
The fountains of a little peace
Splash heavy brittle tears. The years
Wrinkle the stubborn foreheads of these hills

This wet evening, in a lost age.

Southend at Dusk

The unobtrusive trampships gather
Dull-leaden, loaded, spaced across the bay
– Each with a fat hydrogenous amiable angel –
And let the night's vague kindness come their way.

'Say! What's it like beyond the Kentish Knock?'
– The barmaid dreams from a window on the Pier.
'I'd know your step in a million on my stair.
Do you still dream of me? Or don't you care, my dear?'

Alongside the esplanade the fishshops stink.
Stumbling from cut-glass lounges, cursing all
The bleeding universe that drowns the taste
For beer within the stronger taste for drink,
The men in khaki lift inflated heads
And wink and drift ballooning to their beds.

'Oh won't you answer from the Kentish Knock?
Is it another world than this one here?
Or do your thoughts still foul me, even there?
Has the salt water changed your ways, my dear?'

The soiled and broken windows lose their glint.
The four-point-fives are growling on the cape.
Enraged by the reckless tourists of the Night
The metal is alive. Who shall escape?

A murmur comes from all the tangled streams:
'We cannot change our ways. Though we can tame
The sea, we cannot curb our plunging dreams.
Man has no master: no one takes the blame.
Each drinks the other to a lucky end.
More than the sea we fear our pride and shame.'
And who shall count the bony fragile heads
Of every mother's son who knew despair
For one fierce drowning moment, till he sank
Beneath the shifting tides, and did not care?

'Oh why does my heart no longer leap
When men come creaking up my stair?
Oh why do I feel so *mean*, so *mean*?'

'Oh, snip the flowers, Molly. Go to sleep.
I tell you, by the Christ, there's no one there.'

Greetings

The aeroplane engines in my head,
The field guns barking in my side
Fade in the lunar vagueness of a sickbed;
My hands are empty in the void.

Only there stands by the curtained pane
The gaunt insomniac wish to understand
Within my clenched and swollen mind
This white unknown Creation that surprises
Because its silences are kind.

But I am anxious, in this silence,
For you, my everlasting friend.
For in the rain, three nights ago, I heard
The scurry of death, and I saw you bend
Convulsed in darkness, clutching a sudden wound.
I saw your eyes distend.

I know that many a laughing boy
Tonight the Libyan sand devours
And fly-blown eyes that knew the dance
Are glazed with the tale of infinite hours.

But may you lie where nurses mark the graph
Above the bruised indifferent heads
Of men on whom the world no more depends –
While new formations hold the fragile threads
Of power and of glory and dominion,
They lie miasmic on their wintry beds.

So I send, dear friend, a palpable greeting
By airgraph, phrasing the human anonymous wish,
That many shall spring where one has died
And the sour cells of the suffering
Receive small gifts the angels do not sing
And only the arrogant heart has denied.

For look, beyond two thousand circling years
The swaying lanterns glow
Within the moist breath of the muddy cattle
About a miracle the children know:

A light within the chaos of God's mind; –

But how can this small greeting find
A way through all that timeless space
If you have gone, and left no word behind?

Prelude and Fugue

My grandfather had ploughed his master's land;
My father had the ancestral peace of mind,
My mother had the dance in her,
The deep despair and the unbounded hope;
But passionate loyalty betrayed her ways
And such complexity tied down her tongue
That she kept silent long, yet not too long.
For when at last she spoke her words had wisdom,
Both she and I have had the dream of darkness –
Of darkness beating implacably into the brain
Of the preacher unheeded and pitiful on the hillside,
And the poor no different for all his anguish.

My brother wanted to play Rugger for Wales.
He took nothing seriously, and least himself.
He twisted to his own ways, both women and bad luck.
My sister had always desired to be herself
As a young foal or a lonely seagull
When the wind is wild on the sea pastures –
And she also dreamed of the darkness.

But from a greater distance, and even more deeply
She came, half-willed, half-willing, the beautiful stranger
Ashamed of her own compulsion, dreading my vision
Yet beating my gaze down, returning all my wonder.
'You have come to the sacrament?' I said.
'I am the wine,' she answered, 'and the bread.'

And now that the darkness is throbbing through all the
        desolate lands
Where the dead must bury the dead who still prolong
Their bitter argument; where love cries out
A country's or a woman's name in vain;
Where the armoured monsters tremble, but not with pity,
And rumble inexorably onwards, into the dream of
        darkness,
I inherit my father's peace, my mother's silence,

And everything is as one. The beautiful stranger
Is singing the songs in which the larks are hidden –
That music was always in us, farmer, collier, or sailor.

What seemed a long way is not far to go.

On Leave: Marriage

As we left the highroad and sped dimly
Through the peninsula of failing light,
We glimpsed soft sights which stirred us like premonitions:
The brindled backs of cows in candle-lit byres,
Tea laid in parlours by the side of streams,
Curlews and whitewashed farms and the ploughman's gear,
Walls of sea-whitened stones baulking the furze-land,
Great promontories nesting in silence, and brooding black
in the dusk
A ruined ivy-covered keep
And Kerry ewes nibbling the mangold heap.

We folded the ordnance map, in view of this more convincing
evidence.
And when we knocked at the door, the lean woman knew
our names.
She showed us our bedroom with a view of the sea.

But we could not believe it, nor be glad of each other,
And leaving the fireside went out into the rain
Where the ecstasy of blackbirds quickened the thorny hedge
And gulls screamed at the Atlantic from a perilous ledge.

Then only, knowing that moment,
Mouth on mouth, spirit and flesh at one,
We fused the eternal stars with the touch of time.
And our lips were salt and swollen with tears that cried
Love's unavailing truth to rock and star,
Denying evil, plague and death and war.

Sonnet (aboard a troopship) To Gweno

A new occasion like a star has risen
Though all we knew and valued has declined
Below the unattainable horizon
Whose cornfields swish in every landless mind.

But life insists; and this harsh moment knows
Life's envoys from their very absence ride
With whispered promise of a new repose
And you are there, beloved, at my side.

Opening the narrow doors of history,
Moulding each failure to a newer grace,
Interpreting the broken mystery
Of each unguarded malleable face.

For you who feared not love fear not to go
Where knives give bitter blow on counter-blow.

Letter From The Cape

I

Across seven thousand miles of sea and time,
Mererid, you are frightened for our lives,
Frightened of the luminous leisurely
Nibbling carrion of the sunken hives,
Frightened of the silence of the sea
And of the scuffling knives.

II

Yet we are safely at this port of call,
Hurrying down the gangway with our passes;
Street cars run to town and rickshaw boys
Know the brothels and the cost of masses.

Petrol and powder burn this sudden land,
The women's breasts are bare and black as tar,
The skins of crocodile and bat
Hang with dry seaweed in the black bazaar.

The alleyways grow warm with dark,
And there is some grey horror there.
They are doing something horrible to a *man* –
Scuffling, stabbing, sobbing with despair.

We thought we'd sailed beyond the proper bounds
Of our traditional and legal hate,
But here the mood lies deeper than the blade,
And rancour breeds a harsh consumptive fate.

In each green humid esplanade,
Each suncracked parching wall,
The crickets' shrill metallic buzz
Ignores what must befall.

III

I send you a Christmas present, sweet,
A cheap kimono packed
In coloured string and paper
And the love you never lacked

And never feared, though drugged and dragged,
Engulfed and disabused and cast aside
By the green force, the blind unwilling
Tide that compels the bridegroom and the bride.

IV

And now we seek once more the burning breeze,
The sea's indifference and its chances,
The corpses bleaching on a raft,
The zone where the red crab prances;

Yet do not fear, beloved,
Though fear is close as breath,
The knives, the night, the silence of the sea,
Nor even death.

For we are bound by such affinity
Who hear the beating of each other's heart,
That those three huntsmen, Love and Life and Death,
Seek but one quarry, not two beasts apart.

V

And still the heart breaks, wakeful all the night?
Its wisdom cries against its helplessness,
Weary of patience and the world's demands,
And grief that never asks redress.

Yet cast out fear, for fear destroys your flame,
And let your heart lie quiet in your breast.
For I shall come again, in some strange shape,
And you shall turn the key, my sweet, and rest.

Bequest

Tonight this anguish hurts my hands,
This Eucharist I cannot see,
Your pale distressing image in my grasp,
And I must speak, though clumsily,

Of the thorn trees in the lane,
My father stooping at the door,
Soling my boots or clipping my coarse hair,
And never hinting we were poor;

My uncle trudging coal-black from the pit
With such transcendent music in his head
I heard the stars all singing
The night that he lay dead;

And that quick-tempered chapel man
Who loved the sea and all its gear,
He had a broken house, and a trim yacht,
And lived in mysteries and did not fear.

And these recur and I am glad
That they have lived and died
Within my blood and will live on
Whatever may betide.

I leave you in their company,
The winter snow heaped on your door,
In the dark house in the mountains
With a robin on the floor.

And yours are the mysteries
Of Love and Life and Death.
But I, in what remains, only recall
Your beauty quickening my breath.

The Suicide

The end came suddenly for him.
He ran away until he lost his breath,
Then sat in a Soho restaurant
Considering the trick of death.

'Hors d'oeuvres, tornedos, compotes de fraise' –
A bit incongruous, such a thought –
He did not want a carafe of *vin rouge*.
Last suppers cost a lot more than they ought.

No Cockney happened to make him laugh.
No girl in pyjamas gave him a little look.
And none but the officials want his name
To make an entry in a book.

* * * * *

Why such a harsh reply to his request?
Why was the mortgage so abruptly closed?
Why was he so alone in a People's Age?
He could have hitched a lift, you'd have supposed.

It is the damnable Too Much;
The public battened on his private pain,
And he would take no respite from
The immaculate Gestapo of his brain.

He would not make our Cause his own;
He slipped through every clause in every plan –
Yet he who wouldn't tie two bits of string
Now lies serene and serious as a Man.

The River Temple: Wai

The minnows leap like silver coins
In the hard steel water by the reeds
Where buffaloes lie basking in the shallows
And the bald old priest with wizened loins
Fouls his net among the weeds.

The woman in the blue frayed sari
Places a brimming pitcher on her head.
The priest is cleaning out his mesh.
A bell rings in the temple, words are said.
And should the gleaming pitcher fall
The ancient curse will start afresh.
Some vital impetus is dead.

The mountains falter and the evening
Lapses in a flight of geese,
The squirming wicker basket full of minnows
Holds more comfort than the gods.
The woman makes obeisance to the priest.

The soldier squatting like a peasant
Soothes his fever in the stream,
And in the sterile fires of this land
He sees as in a dream
English pastures rank and pleasant,
The primrose woods all cupped with snow,
A girl in an hotel bedroom –

Oh take your rifle up and go
The peasant has his certainties, but you
Must seek beyond religion's gloom
The love the violent do not know,
Compassion of the holy womb.

The Run-In

Two hours after midnight she was in her proper position,
And heaving-to she lowered the landing craft from their derricks,
Soundlessly almost with oil on the blocks and purchase.
And she opened her sally ports and the troops filed up from the
    mess-decks, softly in their heavy boots in the dingy blue lights,
And filed quietly each one to his appointed place.
And all the actions they had rehearsed so often now were slightly
    heightened,
And the look of simplicity or anxiety or ignorance on their faces,
    that also was slightly heightened
In the dingy blue light, still sleepy, newly awakened.
One man hunched in the bows, he was given to dreaming.
Some aesthetic passionate impulse always moved him to consider
    the fitness of things.
He was contemplating this operation against the enemy, and
    thinking.

    Always when I wake there is a little wind on my skin and
    I sweat and cannot find any consolation and cannot tell
    What point in the universe I am. There is no retention.
    Life transfers itself; the dead have friendships with the living,
    And the living often hold their profoundest loyalties with the
        dead.
    And most of us owe something both to the dead and the living,
        and move almost unconsciously between worlds.
    Yet when I have this waking dejection, not knowing whether
    I am really alive or dead, then I am saddened,
    Although they are both expressions of the same experience
    Of dying and living.
    Sadness is an emotion, and the emotions are sad
    Because you dare not try to hold love any more,
    And the lover is always elsewhere than the beloved.
    And always there is the rude itch of the present,
    And the ghostly infidelity of the past never relenting
    And you betray again and again all the deep and comforting
    beliefs of your particular genius, that is to say your childhood,
    And you defer writing letters and you choose what to say.

And even that beautiful morning when two black robins were singing
And contemplating themselves in my mirror and defiling my books with their droppings and exquisitely singing,
Even then the old ghost was there.

The only thing to do is yield to the motion of the boat, and the man next to him, if you want to avoid being seasick.
The engine was purring and there was the slight nausea of petrol,
Their faces uptilted and luminous in the dark well of the craft,
The water was slapping over the square ramp in the bows
And they were steering dead into the pole star, with the plough tilting down on them, their familiar.

And this other man he enjoyed a good film with Betty Grable,
And Akim Tamiroff he liked, or Abbot and Costello,
Or listening to Troise and his mandoliers playing a Tzigane or a Czardas,
And he was thinking among other things of the women where they'd been stationed, he had no affection for virgins,
And he was thinking he'd be starving tomorrow night on the meagre ration they carried, especially if they had such close fighting, that made you hungry.
And he said This life is a mucking muckup, and you don't know where you are from one day to the next, nor what it's all about, nor nothing.
How far is this bleeding coastline, anything's better than fishing.
And he thought it'll be Tee Kye if all the Japs are sleeping.
And gradually they noticed the stars paling, and becoming slowly ineffectual, one after one, the stars paling, the greyness growing.
And each of them knew it was coming.
And the dreamer thought that in other latitudes men and women
Were going about the lawful business of copulation
In very respectable houses and he was thinking
Et ego in Arcadia vixi.
The man next to him was also thinking of his missus

195

And how in the summer there were dahlias on the kitchen table.
And peeping over the benches they saw at last the disturbing
 mountains,
Breaking the calm unattainable quiet horizon.
And then the rocks and the long thin beaches, and the sparse red
 soil sloping up from the beaches,
The palm trees casually isolated, naked long boles and the long
 coarse leaves in limp clusters.
And it was somehow just as one had always imagined it,
The fawn hill and the narrow pink beaches and the desultory
 testimony of the palms,
Some place – even at home you were haunted – but once there
 was always a home.
For a moment it was unbearably poignant.
And now running in on a final throw of the engine,
Cutting out, coasting, still, its seems, holding surprise,
You have difficulty in breathing,
And at last the shock of beaching, hitting the real wetness of the
 sand,
And you leap over the falling ramp and plunge kneedeep, your
 nailed boots sinking
Deep in the yielding clinging softsands of the land.
Is there no enemy? Is the enemy sleeping?
Who will survive the next minute? Is this another of the
 dreamer's dreams?
The day suddenly becomes violent and staccato with the deadly
 rattle of the Taisho
And the men stumble, everywhere, with the convulsed
 bewildered faces, yes, of children.

Indolence

Like a ringdove fat with sun
Placid monotonous incessant you
In twig nest fouled as soon as done
Coo and coo and coo and coo.

Like a goldfish in a rich man's pool,
Plump and naked, idle, petulant
Your round elastic mouth would play the fool
With all on whom your fishy lust is bent.

I know the utter charm you wield
When feebleness feels male and strong,
The comforting smallness of laughter
Where gravity has pressed too long,

The languor of your soft diversions,
The wild come hither of the gadding night,
The private bed above the public bar,
The warm annuity, the cheap delight,

The passion the police excuse,
The rustle in the envelope, the kiss
That gives the shipwrecked harbour in the tempest
And timeless anguish drugs with instant bliss.

But the heart is harsh with wounds
And you debase its immolation
By your wayside victories
And succeeding desolation.

Luxurious goldfish, stupid dove,
Your pleasure is the beast of love.

The Patrol

The branches murmur with the soft thunder
Of distant surf as the wind rising
Tosses its antlered head.
The sky's veins, intricately interlacing,
Form a pattern the dove perhaps
Knew when it pilfered from sheep's-back,
Farmyard and heath the wool and hair and twigs
And in the sky's ganglion
Made habitation.

What else it knew? – beyond the instinctive comfort
Of home in the sated impulse.
The vague unnerving truth of the uncertain,
The premonition of summer, the leaves folding
Green veils of murmuring coolness all about it,
A mystery its wings may shatter,
Its crooning make articulate?

Or some austerer sense, some intuition
Of horny claws and beak and beady eyes,
A sophist's sudden vast illumination,
Knowledge of its nest's unapproachable height?

Head tilted back, I see it swaying
In the incomprehensible wisdom of heaven
As I continue, cautious step by step,
Slowly, disciplined to anguish,
Stopping my terrified legs from running.

And in my stealth I sense with horror
The imminent murder pierce the maiden film
Of dusk that has dissolved the morning's mountain.
It fades about me like a dying culture.
Sleep then for ever, my dreaming German soldier.

Lady in Black

Lady in black,
I knew your son.
Death was our enemy
Death and his gun.

Death had a trench
And he blazed away.
We took that trench
By the end of the day.

Lady in black
Your son was shot.
He was my mate
And he got it hot.

Death's a bastard
Keeps hitting back.
But a war's a war
Lady in black.

Birth hurt bad
But you didn't mind.
Well maybe Death
Can be just as kind.

So take it quiet
The same as your son.
Death's only a vicar
Armed with a gun.

And one day Death
Will give it back
And then you can speak to him tidy
Lady in black.

Beloved Beware

Before you will it so
Beloved beware,
Is there time for love to grow?
Love is already there.

When you look at me
Do I not answer
As though you were dancing
And I the dancer?

The millrace of the blood
Beats against my smile
And am I answering your smile
Or the millrace of your blood?

Under stress we change.
What book of chemistry
Can tell what forms will grow
From this corporeal mystery?

Only love me if you can
Give what no one else can claim
For the woman and the man
Wither at the touch of shame.

If you lose too much
By loving me, foreswear
All I offer you.
Beloved beware
This you know is true
Love is already there.

Renewal

Tragedy has no curtain.
The spirit mutters and denies
The ashes, the wreaths, the darkness,
The circumstantial lies,

And wears the day's dull dress
And lets his will be done
In hospitals and churches
In this one and another one,

Until the dagger in the heart
And the ghost in the soul
Lean on each other suddenly
And the darkness grows whole,

As the whale in the ocean,
As the beast in the snows,
As everything past contrivance
Relives what it knows,

Matching itself, surviving
The avalanche, the wave,
Out of this chaos wresting
The instinctive trust it gave.

Pastorals

I

Had I ever a young field
In July tenderly thrusting
Rain-filled, strong in yield,
Bearded millet rustling,
In September swaying
Like ponies newly foaled

Not before sowing gold
To usurer and clerk –
Copper for that gold –

Then sons would come in season
Sturdy as the apple tree
Inheriting my land,
And love and pride have reason.
But I stand here instead
With dry earth in my hand,
And death in my head
Crying Treason! Treason!

II

Oh in a slim spaced forest
In a gladed darkness deep
With long rough grasses touching
The night aware and animal
Behold the tawny-eyed
Wild elements conjoin
In the endlessly longed-for mutation
Of decay and generation.

The Soubrettes

The old soubrettes could always dance
And play the little tricks of love
Though clients changed from night to night
They peeled their stockings with a glance

That made a simulacrum of delight
With cocktails and with kisses and surrender,
Levitating gaily in the sham
Unhonoured interplay of lust and spite

Until a boy's spontaneous smile
Strayed on them from another world
And brought the glasses crashing to the floor
And everything grew shrill and vile

And an infernal black abyss
Gaped in the limbo of the kiss.
Between the dreamer and the dream
Is always now a shudder and a scream.

Index of Titles